A New Owner's
Guide to
Alaskan Malamutes

JG-140

Overleaf: Alaskan Malamute adult and puppy, owned by Cheryl Paterson and Sandee Reeves.

Opposite page: Alaskan Malamutes "Muffin" and "Parka," owned by Carolyn Hays.

The Publisher wishes to acknowledge the following owners of the dogs in this book: Alkai Kennels, R. Bedaux, Shilon Bedford, Sandy Cooper, Allison Crouse, Bill and Norma Dudley, Mike and Dorrit Evensen, Mike and Mary Ann Fearns, Bill and Debbie Griffiths, Mark and Susan Hamilton, Carolyn Hays, Al and Mary Jane Holabach, Pat Land, Shirley Matthews, Leann Miller, Gae Minich, Karen Moore, Anna Morelli, Jari and Riitta Nirhamo, Patty Padgett, Dorothy Peterson, Tami Rimple, Brent and Tina Robbins, Raissa Rubenstein, Karen Sanders, Frank and Lyn Sattler, Caprice and Vic Scarano, Sandra and Allen Shallbetter, Julie Simon, Michelle Talalay, Tote-Um Kennels, Warren and Dorothy Unterholzner, Tom and Sally Vogel, Wencinja Alaskan Malamutes, Yukon Kennels.

Photographers: Isabelle Francais, Carolyn Hays, Al and Mary Jane Holabach, Jerry Varva Photography, Joan Smith Photography, Steve Miller, Karen Taylor, Wil de Veer.

The author acknowledges the contribution of Judy Iby for the following chapters: Sport of Purebred Dogs, Health Care, Dental Care, Identification and Finding the Lost Dog and Behavior and Canine Communication.

© **by T.F.H. Publications, Inc.**

A New Owner's Guide to
Alaskan Malamutes

Al and Mary Jane Holabach

Contents

6 · Origin and History of the Alaskan Malamute
Contemporary History • The Klondike Gold Rush

16 · Characteristics of the Alaskan Malamute
Case for the Purebred Dog • Who Should Own an Alaskan Malamute? • Character of the Alaskan Malamute

24 · Official Standard of the Alaskan Malamute
AKC Breed Standard for the Alaskan Malamute • Discussion of the Standard

An Alaskan Malamute demonstrates his wolf ancestry by howling at the moon.

34 · Selecting the Right Malamute for You
What to Look for in a Breeder • What the Breeder Will Want to Know • Health Concerns • Recognizing a Healthy Puppy • Male or Female? • Selecting a Show Prospect Puppy • Puppy or Adult? • Identification Papers • Diet Sheet • Health Guarantee • Temperament and Socialization • The Adolescent Malamute • The Malamute Protection League

56 · Caring for Your Alaskan Malamute
Nutrition • Bathing and Grooming • Exercise • Socialization

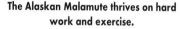

The Alaskan Malamute thrives on hard work and exercise.

72 · Housebreaking and Training
Housebreaking • Basic Training • Versatility

90 · Sport of Purebred Dogs
Puppy Kindergarten • Conformation • Canine Good Citizen • Obedience • Tracking • Agility • Performance Tests • General Information

The love for snow and sledding is inherent in the Alaskan Malamute.

130 · Health Care
The First Check Up • The Physical Exam • Immunizations • Intestinal Parasites • Other Internal Parasites • Heartworm Disease • External Parasites • To Breed or Not to Breed • Medical Problems

148 · Dental Care for Your Dog's Life

156 · Identification and Finding the Lost Dog
Finding the Lost Dog

An Alaskan Malamute is always ready to go with his master.

Mischievous Malamute puppies need to be taught the rules of the household.

110 · Behavior and Canine Communication
Canine Behavior • Socializing and Training • Understanding the Dog's Language • Body Language • Fear • Aggression Problems

ORIGIN and History of the Alaskan Malamute

As the mists of the dawn of civilization began to clear, a relationship between man and a beast of the forest had already begun to form. Man's major pursuits then were simply providing food for himself and his family and protecting the members of the tribe from the many dangers which threatened their existence.

Early man undoubtedly saw his own survival efforts reflected in the habits of this beast that made ever-increasing overtures at coexistence. That beast was none other than *Canis lupus*—the wolf.

The Alaskan Malamute has retained the appearance and many of the characteristics of his wolf-like ancestors.

The road from a wolf in the wild to "man's best friend," *Canis familiaris,* is as long and fascinating as it is fraught with widely varying explanations. However, it seems obvious that observation of the wolf could easily have taught early man some effective hunting skills that he, too, would be able to use advantageously. Wolves saw in man's discards a source of easily secured food. The association grew from there.

The wolves that could assist man in satisfying the unending human need for food were of course most highly prized. It also became increasingly obvious as the man-wolf relationship developed through the ages that certain descendants of these increasingly domesticated wolves could also be used by man to

6

A descendant of the Northern or Arctic branch of the wolf family, the Alaskan Malamute feels at home in the frozen tundra.

assist in survival pursuits other than hunting. Some of these wolves were large enough and strong enough to assist man as a beast of burden. Others were aggressive enough to protect man and the tribe he lived with from danger.

In their enlightening study of the development of dog breeds, *The Natural History of Dogs,* authors Richard and Alice Feinnes classify most dogs as having descended from one of four major groups: the Dingo Group, the Greyhound Group, the Northern Group and the Mastiff Group. Each of these groups trace back to separate and distinct branches of the wolf family.

The Dingo Group traces its origin to the Asian wolf (*Canis lupus pallipes*). Two well-known examples of the Dingo Group are the Basenji and, through the admixture of several European breeds, the Rhodesian Ridgeback.

The Greyhound Group descends from a coursing-type relative of the Asian Wolf. The group includes all those dogs which hunt by sight and are capable of great speed. The Greyhound itself, the Afghan Hound, the Borzoi and Irish Wolfhound are all examples of this group and are known as the coursing breeds. They are not true hounds in that they do not hunt by scent.

The Arctic or Nordic Group of dogs is a direct descendant of the rugged northern wolf (*Canis lupus*). Included in the many breeds of this group are the Alaskan Malamute, Chow Chow, German Shepherd and the much smaller Welsh Corgi and Spitz-type dog.

The fourth classification is the Mastiff Group which owes its primary heritage to the Tibetan wolf (*Canis lupus chanco* or *laniger*). The great diversity of the dogs included in this group indicates they are not entirely of pure blood in that the specific breeds included have undoubtedly been influenced by descendants of the other three groups.

The Northern Group, like their undomesticated ancestors, maintained the characteristics that protect from the harsh environment of the upper European countries. Weather-resistant coats protected from rain and cold. There was a long, coarse outercoat that shed snow and rain and a dense undercoat that insulated against sub-zero temperatures. These coats were especially abundant around the neck and chest, thereby offering double protection for the vital organs.

Well-coated tails could cover and

Originally used as a draft dog to pull sleds, the Malamute thrives on hard work and exercise.

Getting back to his roots, "Boone" owned by Caprice and Vic Scarano overlooks Harbor Mountain in Sitka, Alaska.

protect the nose and mouth should the animal be forced to sleep in the snow. Small prick ears were not as easily frostbitten or frozen as the large and pendulous ear of some of the other breeds. The muzzle had sufficient length to warm the frigid air before it reached the lungs. Leg length was sufficient to keep the chest and abdomen above the snow line. Tails were carried horizontally or up over the back rather than trailing behind in the snow.

Skeletal remains of these early wolf descendants have been found throughout northern and central Europe, northern Asia and the Arctic regions of North America. The group stands as the forerunner of what are also commonly referred to as the Arctic breeds.

This group can be effectually divided into four categories: hunting dogs (examples: Norwegian Elkhound, Chow Chow and Karelian Bear Dog); draft dogs (Alaskan Malamute, Siberian Husky); herding dogs (Samoyed, Swedish and Finnish Lapphunds); and companion dogs (including most of the Spitz-type dogs—German Spitz, Japanese Spitz, Pomeranian, American Eskimo and Volpino Italiano).

Tina Robbins and "Rain Dancer" educate the masses about the breed's rich history by participating in the Alaskan Malamute breed exhibit at the Puyallup Fair in Washington.

This is not to indicate that there were no cross-breedings of the types nor that abilities peculiar to one group may not have been possessed by another. In fact, some historians believe that many of the Northern or Arctic breeds that retain a degree of hunting ability owe this strength to their Asian Dingo type heritage which is absent from other breeds whose ancestors were not exposed to this admixture. It is also believed that this cross provided these Northern breeds with a more refined attitude and tractability.

As the eastward migration of the nomadic tribes from Siberia continued, it eventually crossed the now submerged Bering Land Bridge and brought man and his dogs to Alaska. It is impossible to know exactly when man began to use dogs to assist him in hauling, but it is believed the practice began in northern Eurasia and traveled eastward with the migrating tribes. Certainly the dogs capable of bringing down game as large as elk, moose and caribou would have the strength necessary to assist man in bringing the kill back to the campsite as well.

As the tribes crossed the Bering Strait and scattered themselves through the Alaskan territory, each tribe began to develop the characteristics in their dogs that would prove most beneficial. One such tribe was the Mahlemut Indians that settled throughout the Kotzebue Sound in the upper regions of western Alaska.

The extremely harsh conditions of the territory demanded a dog of dynamic constitution, extraordinary hardiness and great strength. What resulted in ensuing generations was the incredibly powerful dog that would derive its name from the tribe that developed it and the area in which the breed thrived—the Russian-owned land called Alashak or Alyeska. While the meaning of the word Malamute has never been established, it appears "Mahle" is translated from the

Dubbed the "kings of the working breeds," these Alaskan Malamute pups get acquainted with their sled.

Eskimo language to mean "of the people."

The Mahlemut Indians lived in a remote and rugged environment. They needed a multi-faceted dog, one that possessed the skill of the hunter, the maneuverability of the herder and the strength and endurance of the draught dog. The dogs were as strong-minded and strong-willed as their owners. These characteristics distinguish the Alaskan Malamute of today and have earned the breed the title "king of the working breeds."

CONTEMPORARY HISTORY

Explorers through the centuries extolled the virtues of these Mahlemut dogs. Vitus Bering and Otto von Kotzebue conducted early expeditions to Alaska Bering as early as 1680 and Kotzebue through 1846. Both unanimously celebrated Alaskan dogs of great strength and reliability whose unique markings and and beauty of form made them outstanding among all canine breeds.

As explorers and tradesmen found their way to the Alaskan territories, word of the noble beasts bred and owned by the Mahlemut Indians began to spread throughout the world. As early as 1888 a noted dog writer who did all his work under the *nom de plume* Stonehenge wrote of the breed he called "the Esquimaux Dog" in *The Dogs of Great Britain, America and Other Countries*:

The early Alaskan Malamutes were used as working dogs and beasts of burden, a task they still can accomplish today. Sandy Shallbetter hiking with friends Nuka and Ladyhawk.

"These dogs are the only beasts of burden in the northern part of America and the adjacent islands, being sometimes employed to carry materials for hunting or the produce of the chase on their backs. At other times they are harnessed to sledges in teams, varying from 7 to 11, each being capable of drawing a hundred-weight for his share.

The Esquimaux Dog is about 22 or 23 inches high. . . Siberian and Greenland dogs are nearly similar to those of Kamtschatka, but somewhat larger, and also more manageable all being used in the same way. The dog common to the region of the Saskatchewan River and Lake Winnipeg is stone-grey, of large and bony build, with large spreading feet and with prick ears... It has a heavy jaw, very small round ears, which are always erect, and the hair, which is long, hard and wiry,

invariably stands erect off the skin, very similar to that of a bear, to which the whole dog bears a very close resemblance when lying down."

Alaskan Malamute puppies romping in the snow!

Early explorers to Alaska also wrote enthusiastically of these native dogs. According to the *Alaska Geographic Quarterly*, Henry M. Bannister, who headed an Alaskan expedition from 1865-1867, found these dogs incredibly anxious to perform their duties at the sled: "As soon as the sled is brought out... the dogs gather round, and, fairly dancing with excitement, raise their voices in about a dozen unmelodious strains."

The isolated Mahlemute people needed a dog that could haul their goods long distances. The strength to pull and the structure lending itself to endurance were far more important than speed, and their dogs reflected these needs with great size, powerful physiques and incredible endurance.

THE KLONDIKE GOLD RUSH

When the Klondike Gold Rush began in 1896, the serviceability and endurance, as well as the beauty of the Alaskan Malamute, created an unprecedented demand for the breed. Because it became impossible to fulfill these demands, cross-breedings and "look-alikes" were offered, but none could command the respect of a purebred Alaskan Malamute team. For this reason, those who had Malamutes of pure breeding guarded these bloodlines jealously and protected the dogs from the contamination of other breeds.

In the early 1900s the American purebred dog fancy took some notice of the breed, which was then legendary among Alaskans, but it was with mild enthusiasm. A club for the breed was not to be organized until 1935, but in the interim breed enthusiasts were actively building a foundation for an additional path for the breed to follow— that of a home companion and show dog.

In 1929 a US-born litter sired by Yukon Jad out of a female named Bessie produced four males. Among them was a dog who was to become a legend in the breed. His name was Gripp of Yukon, and he not only became the first Alaskan Malamute ever to be registered with the American Kennel Club he was also to become the breed's first recorded champion anywhere in the world.

In 1935 the Alaskan Malamute Club (later, the Alaskan Malamute Club of America) was formed for the advancement and protection of the breed. The breed was given full recognition by the American Kennel Club in that same year.

Also, by this time the dog fancy at large had learned the Alaskan Malamute was an extremely kind and gentle dog and began to realize that, looks aside, the Malamute had none of the characteristics of its ancient ancestor, the wolf. Ongoing research and interviews with Eskimos were to prove time and time again that once the breed had established itself thousands of years before, there were no known wolf crosses made by intent or by accident.

Without a doubt, much of the credit for the development and recognition of the breed by the AKC must be given to Mrs. Eva Seeley. Mrs. Seeley was the breeder and owner of Gripp of Yukon and she campaigned Gripp and several other Malamutes from her Chinook Kennels to bring the breed to public attention and to obtain American Kennel Club recognition. Gripp also served as the model for the first AKC breed standard.

Over the years, the Malamute has retained his ruggedness and love of the outdoors—especially after a good snow.

The first Alaskan Malamute to win a Working Group in the United States was Ch. Mulpus Brooks the Bear, who was given the award by judge William Kendrick in 1954. It was not until 1963 that Ch. Sno-Crest's Mukluk was to break the Best In Show barrier for the Alaskan Malamute when he was owner-handled to the award by Martha Guiffre.

True Malamute fanciers have never ignored the breed's origins and continued to compete in sled dog races both in the United States and in Alaska. Alaska, long known as "Seward's Icebox," became one of the United States in 1959.

The Alaskan Malamute has done nothing but gain in popularity and respect since those early days. Breeders have done a remarkable job to maintain the breed's sterling qualities and stabilize its temperament and reliability. The breed has become a trusted and reliable member of thousands of households throughout the world without losing its great courage and independence.

CHARACTERISTICS of the Alaskan Malamute

If you are still in the "deciding" stage of whether or not you should bring an Alaskan Malamute puppy into your life, we caution that you do not—and we repeat, *do not* —visit a kennel or home in which there are Malamute puppies. You will not leave without one! Malamute puppies are absolutely irresistible. Of all the breeds we have known in our lives, none is so captivating as the baby Alaskan Malamute.

It is for this very reason that the person anticipating owning an Alaskan Malamute should give serious thought to the decision. All puppies are picture-postcard cuddly and cute, Malamute puppies particularly so. The Alaskan Malamute, however, may not really be a dog for the first-time dog owner. This will become clear as the unique character of the breed is revealed.

All puppies are irresistible and Malamutes are certainly no exception. How do you choose just one?

There is nothing more seductive than a litter of fluffy little puppies, nestled together sound asleep, one on top of the other. But in addition to being cute, puppies are living, breathing and very mischievous little creatures, and they are entirely dependent upon their human owner for *everything* once they leave their mother and littermates. Further, the fluffy and dependent puppy quickly becomes a lean machine of activity whose adolescent hormones continuously rage and inspire relentless activity.

Buying a dog, especially a puppy, before someone is absolutely sure he wants to make that commitment can be a serious mistake. The prospective dog owner must clearly understand the amount of time and work involved in dog

Carefully consider the responsibilities of dog ownership before deciding to bring an Alaskan Malamute puppy home.

ownership. Failure to understand the extent of commitment dog ownership involves is one of the primary reasons there are so many unwanted canines that end their lives in an animal shelter.

Before anyone contemplates the purchase of a dog, there are some very important conditions that must be considered. One of the first questions that must be answered is whether or not the person who will ultimately be responsible for the dog's care and well being actually wants a dog.

All too often it is the mother of the household who must shoulder the responsibility of the family dog's day-to-day care. While the children in the family, perhaps even the father, may be wildly enthusiastic about having a dog, it must be remembered they are away most of the day at school or at work. It is often "mom" who will be taking on the additional responsibility of primary care giver for the family dog.

Pets are a wonderful method of teaching children responsibility, but it should be remembered the enthusiasm that inspires children to promise anything in order to have a new puppy may quickly wane. Who will take care of the puppy once the novelty wears off? *Does that person want a dog?*

Desire to own a dog aside, does the lifestyle of the family actually provide for responsible dog ownership? If the entire family is away from home from early morning to late at night, who will provide for all of a puppy's needs? Feeding, exercise, outdoor access and the like cannot be provided if no one is home.

Another important factor to consider is whether or not the breed of dog is suitable for the person or the family with which it will be living. Some breeds can handle the rough-and-tumble play of young children. Some cannot. On the other hand, some dogs are so large and clumsy, especially as puppies, that they could easily and unintentionally injure an infant.

Then, too, there is the matter of hair. A luxuriously coated dog is certainly beautiful to behold, but all that hair takes a great deal of care. In the case of an Alaskan Malamute, an occasional quick pass over with a brush will not suffice. Brushing an adult Malamute requires time and a great deal of elbow grease. Both long- and short-haired dogs shed their coats in the home. Naturally, the longer the hair, the more noticeable it will be and the more apt it will be to carry what seems like half the outdoors into the house after a day's outing.

As great as claims are for any breed's intelligence and

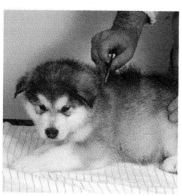

trainability, remember the new dog must be taught every household rule that it is to observe. Some dogs catch on more quickly than others and puppies are just as

The time and care you wish to spend on grooming should be a consideration when choosing a pet.

18

The Alaskan Malamute has a number of unique qualities that make him a friendly and versatile breed.

inclined to forget or disregard lessons as young human children.

CASE FOR THE PUREBRED DOG

As previously mentioned, all puppies are cute. Not all puppies grow up to be particularly attractive adults. What is considered beauty by one person is not necessarily seen as attractive by another. It is almost impossible to determine what a mixed-breed puppy will look like as an adult. Nor will it be possible to determine if the mixed-breed puppy's temperament is suitable for the person or family who wishes to own it. If the puppy grows up to be too big, too hairy or too active for the owner, what then will happen to it?

Size and temperament can vary to a degree even within a purebred breed. Still, selective breeding over many generations has produced dogs giving the would-be owner reasonable assurance of what the purebred puppy will look and act like as an adult. Points of attractiveness completely aside, this predictability is more important than one might think.

A person who wants a dog to go along on those morning jogs or long-distance runs is not going to be particularly happy with a lethargic or short-legged breed. Nor is the fastidious housekeeper, whose picture of the ideal dog is one that lies quietly at the feet of its master by the hour and never sheds, going to be particularly happy with the shaggy dog whose temperament is reminiscent of a hurricane.

Purebred puppies will grow up to look like their adult relatives and, by and large, they will behave pretty much like the rest of their family. Any dog, mixed breed or not, has the potential to be a loving companion. However, a purebred dog offers reasonable insurance that it will suit not only the owner's lifestyle but the person's esthetic demands as well.

WHO SHOULD OWN AN ALASKAN MALAMUTE?

What kind of person should own an Alaskan Malamute? Two words will describe the person: patient and committed. If the Malamute owner is patient in dealing with the developing youngster, he or she will be rewarded with a life companion

The Alaskan Malamute is a athletic breed that welcomes lots of exercise and loves the outdoors. Muffin enjoys her very first snowfall.

whose devotion knows no end and whose sense of humor knows no bounds. However, it takes true commitment and determination to get through to the often stubborn Malamute puppy.

If molding a dog's spirit to conform to your picture of the ideal canine companion is an important factor in dog ownership, consider a breed other than the Alaskan Malamute. Historically, the Malamute has been an independent survivor. You can guide a Malamute in the direction you want it to go but you can't push it there. Nor can you be heavy handed. As tough as the breed may be, he will not tolerate abuse.

As sturdy a constitution as the Alaskan Malamute may have and as high as its tolerance for discomfort might be, a Malamute is completely incapable of withstanding being struck in anger. This devastates the Malamute, and if subjected to treatment of this nature on a continuing basis, it can turn even the most amiable youngster into a neurotic and unpredictable adult.

This is not to say the Malamute owner needs to or should be passive in raising and training his or her dog. On the contrary, a young Malamute must start understanding household rules from the first moment it comes into your home. What it will take to accomplish this is

A purebred Malamute puppy will grow up to look just like his adult relatives and will usually possess a similar temperament.

the aforementioned patience and a firm but gentle and unrelenting hand. Somehow even the youngest Malamute puppy understands the difference between being corrected and being abused.

Someone who needs a dog that does well living outdoors with minimal owner interaction should in all fairness also look for another breed. The Malamute must have constant human companionship and social interaction not only with his owner but with all kinds of people and other dogs. The Malamute raised without this socialization can easily become aggressive and sullen. The young Malamute can pass through an adolescent stage where he decides he will attempt to assert himself by growling at you unless made to understand this is absolutely unacceptable.

It is then up to the caring owner to help guide the Malamute through this difficult stage. Patience, persistence and support will help your Malamute grow through his many difficult stages of development, and it does take time and a commitment to stay on top of the situation with the Malamute puppy that continually questions who is in charge.

Needless to say, the Alaskan Malamute owner must be prepared to take care of the breed's coat. The heavier the coat and the larger the dog, the more time and effort will be required. This is particularly so when the Malamute begins to shed. While tangles and matting are are not a problem in the mature Malamute with the proper coat, the shedding does continue on a semiannual basis. The responsible owner should allow an hour or so at least once a week for general coat and health care.

CHARACTER OF THE ALASKAN MALAMUTE

The Malamute character is as unique as it is contradictory. The breed is extremely clean and, despite the Malamute's size, he makes a wonderful house dog. Housebreaking usually takes half the time of many other breeds. It's a lesson the Malamute seems to want to learn, and once learned only a major catastrophe can get the adult to transgress.

On the other hand, the breed has a stubborn streak a mile long. The experienced Malamute owner knows how quickly the average Malamute understands what you are trying to teach him. The same owner also knows how long it can be before the understanding Malamute chooses to comply.

The breed is not difficult to train because he is so smart, but Malamutes are not particularly dedicated to pleasing their owners. The Malamute has a strong, dominant character and this stubbornness extends itself to how and what he learns. Avoid like the plague the development of bad habits. Once learned, it takes the devil to pay before you will be able to convince your Malamute to forget that bad habit.

Malamute puppies are extremely mischievous, devout chewers and can be very destructive. Never put anything beyond the Malamute puppy's ingenuity or his ability to land right in the middle of a difficult situation!

Your Malamute puppy will love you madly but will not think twice about "arguing" with you over obeying a rule or being corrected. *Puppy growls are not cute!* The Malamute puppy is testing the waters and is trying to determine just who in the family is the "pack leader," you or him.

The first time this happens, we correct the puppy by holding the ruff on both sides of his face, looking him directly in the eye and in a very commanding voice saying, "Enough!" or "Stop!" If you make a strong enough impression, it is highly unlikely that the puppy will forget. Usually this kind of correction is enough, but do not be surprised to find the puppy challenging you in another situation.

Malamute puppies cannot be allowed to grow up lacking controlled socialization with both humans and other animals. It is important this socialization begins very early in the puppy's life and continues on through adolescence.

Have we made Malamute ownership sound like a challenge? If so, you have definitely taken our message. There is no doubt at all that a Malamute will be able to test you in every way possible, but we are inclined to believe it is all done to determine whether or not you are worthy of being a Malamute owner. If you do qualify, you will have a companion the likes of which you will never forget.

Malamute puppies are mischievous, stubborn and can sometimes be destructive. As soon as you bring him home, teach your puppy the rules of the household.

STANDARD of the Alaskan Malamute

General Appearance–The Alaskan Malamute, one of the oldest Arctic sled dogs, is a powerful and substantially built dog with a deep chest and strong, well-muscled body. The Malamute stands well over the pads, and this stance gives the appearance of much activity and a proud carriage, with head erect and eyes alert showing interest and curiosity. The head is broad. Ears are triangular and erect when alerted. The muzzle is bulky, only slight diminishing in width from root to nose. The muzzle is not pointed or long, yet not stubby. The coat is thick with a coarse guard coat of sufficient length to protect a woolly undercoat. Malamutes are of various colors. Face markings are a distinguishing feature. These consist of a cap over the head, the face either all white or marked with a bar and/or mask. The tail is well furred, carried over the back, and has the appearance of a waving plume.

Authors Mary Jane and Al Holabach pose proudly with one of their outstanding examples of the breed.

The Malamute must be a heavy boned dog with sound legs, good feet, deep chest and powerful shoulders, and have all of the other physical attributes necessary for the efficient performance of his job. The gait must be steady, balanced, tireless and totally efficient. He is not intended as a racing sled dog designed to compete in speed trials. The Malamute is structured for strength and endurance, and any characteristic of the individual specimen, including temperament, which interferes with the accomplishment of this purpose, is to be considered the most serious of faults.

Size, Proportion, Substance–There is a natural range in size in the breed. The desirable freighting sizes are males, 25 inches at the shoulders, 85 pounds; females, 23 inches at the shoulders, 75 pounds. However, size consideration should not outweigh that of type, proportion, movement and other

24

functional attributes. When dogs are judged equal in type, proportion, movement, the dog nearest the desirable freighting size is to be preferred. The depth of chest is approximately one half the height of the dog at the shoulders, the deepest point being just behind the forelegs. The length of the body from point of shoulder to the rear point of pelvis is longer than the height of the body from ground to top of the withers. The body carries no excess weight, and bone is in proportion to size.

Head–The head is broad and deep, not coarse or clumsy, but in proportion to the size of the dog. The expression is soft and indicates an affectionate disposition. The *eyes* are obliquely placed in the skull. Eyes are brown, almond shaped and of medium size. Dark eyes are preferred. *Blue Eyes are a Disqualifying Fault.* The *ears* are of medium size, but small in proportion to the head. The ears are triangular in shape and slightly rounded at the tips. They are set wide apart on the outside back edges of the skull on line with the upper corner of the eye, giving ears the appearance, when erect, of standing off from the skull. Erect ears point slightly forward, but when the dog is at work, the ears are sometimes folded against the skull. High set ears are a fault.

The *skull* is broad and moderately rounded between the ears, gradually narrowing and flattening on top as it approaches the eyes, rounding off to cheeks that are moderately flat. There is a slight furrow between the eyes. The topline of the skull and the topline of the muzzle show a slight break downward from a straight line as they join. The *muzzle* is large and bulky in proportion to the size of the skull, diminishing slightly in width and depth from junction with the

Four brunettes and a redhead– the Alaskan Malamute's coat can come in many different colors.

skull to the nose. In all coat colors, except reds, the *nose, lips,* and *eye rims' pigmentation* is black. Brown is permitted in red dogs. The lighter streaked "snow nose" is acceptable. The lips are close fitting. The upper and lower jaws are broad with large teeth. The incisors meet with a scissors grip. Overshot or undershot is a fault.

The Alaskan Malamute should possess an alert, intelligent and friendly expression.

Neck, Topline, Body—The neck is strong and moderately arched. The chest is well developed. The body is compactly built but not short coupled. The back is straight and gently sloping to the hips. The loins are hard and well muscled. A long loin that may weaken the back is a fault. The tail is moderately set and follows the line of the spine at the base. The tail is carried over the back when not working. It is not a snap tail or curled tight against the back, nor is it short furred like a fox brush. The Malamute tail is well furred and has the

The Malamute has a broad head with erect triangular ears and characteristic facial markings that distinguish the breed.

appearance of a waving plume.

Forequarters–The shoulders are moderately sloping; forelegs heavily boned and muscled, straight to the pasterns when viewed from the front. Pasterns are short and strong and slightly sloping when viewed from the side. The feet are of the snowshoe type, tight and deep, with well-cushioned pads, giving a firm, compact appearance. The feet are large, toes tight fitting and well arched. There is a protective growth of hair between the toes. The pads are thick and tough; toenails short and strong.

Hindquarters–The rear legs are broad and heavily muscled through the thighs; stifles moderately bent; hock joints are moderately bent and well let down. When viewed from the rear, the legs stand and move true in line with the movement of the front legs, not too close or too wide. Dewclaws on the rear legs are undesirable and should be removed shortly after puppies are whelped.

The overall appearance of the Alaskan Malamute should be of a substantial and powerfully built dog with a well-muscled body.

With his coarse outer coat and thick undercoat, the Alaskan Malamute is well suited to the rigors of outdoor life.

Coat–The Malamute has a thick, coarse guard coat, never long and soft. The undercoat is dense, from one to two inches in depth, oily and woolly. The coarse guard coat varies in length as does the undercoat. The coat is relatively short to medium along the sides of the body, with the length of the coat increasing around the shoulders and neck, down the back, over the rump, and in the breeching and plume. Malamutes usually have a shorter and less dense coat during the summer months. The Malamute is shown naturally. Trimming is not acceptable except to provide a clean cut appearance of feet.

Color–The usual colors range from light gray through intermediate shadings to black, sable, and shadings of sable to red. Color combinations are acceptable in undercoats, points, and trimmings. The only solid color allowable is all white. White is always the predominant color on underbody, parts of legs, feet, and part of face markings. A white blaze on the forehead and/or collar or a spot on the nape is attractive and acceptable. The Malamute is mantled, and broken colors extending over the body or uneven splashing are undesirable.

Gait—The gait of the Malamute is steady, balanced, and powerful. He is agile for his size and build. When viewed from the side, the hindquarters exhibit strong rear drive that is transmitted through a well-muscled loin to the forequarters. The forequarters receive the drive from the rear with a smooth reaching stride. When viewed from the front or from the rear, the legs move true in line, not too close or too wide. At a fast trot, the feet will converge toward the centerline of the body. A stilted gait, or any gait that is not completely efficient and tireless, is to be penalized.

Temperament—The Alaskan Malamute is an affectionate, friendly dog, not a "one man" dog. He is a loyal, devoted companion, playful in invitation, but generally impressive by his dignity after maturity.

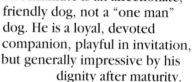

Kiana, owned by Brent and Tina Robbins, is a striking example of a red Alaskan Malamute.

Summary—
IMPORTANT: In judging Malamutes, their function as a sledge dog for heavy freighting in the Arctic must be given consideration above all else. The degree to which a dog is penalized should depend upon the extent to which the particular fault would actually affect the working ability of the dog. The legs of the Malamute just indicate unusual strength and tremendous propelling power. Any indication of unsoundness in legs and feet, front or rear, standing or moving, is to be considered a serious fault. Faults under this provision would be splay-footedness, cowhocks, bad pasterns, straight shoulders, lack of angulation, stilted gait (or any gait that isn't balanced, strong and steady), ranginess, shallowness, ponderousness, lightness of bone, and poor overall proportion.

Ch. Williwaw's Seahawk of Targhee, owned by Mary Jane and Al Holabach, was the number one female Alaskan Malamute.

DISQUALIFICATION: *Blue Eyes*.
Approval Date: April 12, 1994
Effective Date: May 31, 1994

DISCUSSION OF THE STANDARD

The standard of the Alaskan Malamute is written in a simple and straightforward manner that can be read and understood by even the beginning fancier. It takes many years, however, to fully grasp all of the standard's implications. This can only be accomplished through observation of many Malamutes and reading as much about the breed as possible. What follows is meant to assist the beginning fancier to develop a sense of the true character of the breed.

There are some breeds that change drastically from

puppyhood to adulthood. It would be extremely difficult for the novice to determine the actual breed of some dogs in puppyhood, as purebred as the puppies might be. This is not so with the Alaskan Malamute. The really top-quality Malamute puppy can reflect in miniature what it will look like as an adult.

There are many physical characteristics that the Northern breeds share; therefore, their differences become very important in distinguishing one breed from another. This is particularly so in respect to the Alaskan Malamute and the Siberian Husky. The beautiful markings and wide range of colors in both breeds tend to blur the lines a bit at first glance.

Tug, owned by Shirley Matthews, is a shining example of the breed. His outstanding quality made it possible for him to be the top winner in 1977.

The Alaskan Malamute is not only larger and more powerful than the Siberian Husky, it is unquestionably the most imposing of all the Northern breeds. Size and power are in fact hallmarks of this breed, whose origins are based upon a desire and ability to haul heavy loads. It should be remembered, however, that size alone is not indicative of strength, and it is the latter that must never be lost sight of.

Eye color is another characteristic that separates the Malamute from its distant Siberian cousin. The Malamute has warm brown eyes—the darker the better—while the Husky can have brown or blue eyes or even one of each color!

It is not only in size that the Malamute stands above the other northern breeds. The Malamute has far greater bone and substance than any of them. This is reflected in body, head and leg size.

The standard makes a point of describing the Malamute tail as being much different than the Siberian Husky's. While the latter has a tail that might well remind one of a huge bottle brush, the Malamute's tail is more like a large plume majestically waving above the dog's back.

The expression of the Alaskan Malamute is very important. Although there is a slight "wolf-like" appearance because of the way they are placed in the skull, the eyes themselves are warm, trustworthy and indicative of the breed's legendary affectionate temperament.

SELECTING The Right Malamute for You

O nce the prospective Alaskan Malamute owner satisfactorily answers all the questions relating to responsible ownership, he or she will undoubtedly want to rush out and purchase a puppy immediately. Take care—do not act in haste. The purchase of any dog is an important step since the well-cared-for dog will live with you for many years. In the case of a Malamute, this could easily be 11 or 12 years, perhaps longer. You will undoubtedly want the dog that will live with you for that length of time to be one you will enjoy.

It is extremely important in this breed, as it is in any large breed of dog, that your Malamute is purchased from a breeder who has earned a reputation over the years for consistently producing dogs that are mentally and physically sound. There are always those who are ready and willing to exploit a breed for financial gain with no thought given to their health or welfare, or to the homes in which the dogs will be living.

The only way a breeder can earn a reputation for quality is through a well-thought-out breeding program in which rigid selectivity is imposed. Selective breeding is aimed at maintaining the virtues of a breed and eliminating genetic weaknesses. This process is time-consuming and costly. Therefore, responsible Alaskan Malamute breeders protect

their investment by providing the utmost in prenatal care for their brood matrons and maximum care and nutrition for the resulting offspring.

Rain Dancer nurses a healthy litter at Williwaw Kennels.

When deciding on puppy, make sure the breeder runs a quality facility and all the dogs are clean, healthy and well taken care of. A six-week-old litter bred by Paul and Michelle Talalay.

Once the puppies arrive, the knowledgeable breeder initiates a well-thought-out socialization process.

The buyer should look for cleanliness in both the dogs and the areas in which the dogs are kept. Cleanliness is the first clue that tells you how much the breeder cares about the dogs he or she owns.

The governing kennel clubs in the different countries of the world maintain lists of local breed clubs and breeders that can lead a prospective dog buyer to responsible breeders of quality stock. Should you not be sure of where to contact a respected breeder in your area, we strongly recommend contacting your local kennel club for recommendations.

There is every possibility a reputable breeder resides in your area who not only will be able to provide the right Alaskan Malamute for you but who will often have both the parents of the puppy on the premises. This gives you an opportunity to

Observe the puppy you are interested in away from his littermates. Choose the puppy with an alert, happy demeanor and healthy appearance.

see firsthand what kind of dogs are in the background of the puppy you are considering. Good breeders are willing not only to have you see their dogs but to inspect the facility in which the dogs are raised as well. These breeders will also be able to discuss problems that exist in the breed with you and and how they deal with these problems.

WHAT THE BREEDER WILL WANT TO KNOW

Do not be surprised if a concerned breeder asks many questions about you and the environment in which your Malamute will be raised. Good breeders are just as concerned with the quality of the homes to which their dogs are going as you, the buyer, are in obtaining a sound and healthy dog.

There are certain places we do not allow our dogs to go.

No Malamute to "wolf-hybrid" breeders: These individuals like to use Malamutes because of some similarities in looks. Wolf-hybrids can be dangerous, unpredictable animals.

No Malamute to a person without a fenced yard: Malamutes wander, and unless there is a fenced yard or securely fenced enclosure, too many accidents can occur.

No Malamute to couples with infants: These people already have their hands full *without* adding another baby to the household—one that you can't take your eyes off of for eight to twelve months. In fact, we will not let our puppies go to homes with children under five years old.

Malamutes are independent and tend to wander—especially curious puppies! They need a secure fenced area to play in.

No Malamute to individuals who breed too frequently: There aren't that many suitable homes for Malamutes.

We screen prospective owners with third-degree aggression. We ask if the person has ever owned a Malamute or any dog in the past. We want to know what made the person decide on a Malamute. We also explain that we do not sell any Malamute as a pet without the buyer agreeing to spay or neuter the dog.

If the prospective buyer answers all questions satisfactorily, we invite them to our home to "talk dogs" and see how they relate to the breed. If this all goes well we put them on our "wait list" or recommend they see another responsible breeder and give them the name and phone numbers of the breeders we recommend.

Our work does not end with the sale of a puppy. We answer thousands of questions over a dog's entire lifetime. We assist novice owners with the new puppy's training. This is a labor of love for us, and the buyer should expect this from whomever he or she buys their Malamute puppy.

Do not think a good Malamute puppy can only come from a large kennel. On the contrary, today many of the best breeders raise dogs in their homes as a hobby. It is important, however, that you not allow yourself to fall into the hands of an irresponsible "backyard breeder." Backyard breeders separate themselves from the hobby breeder through their lack of responsibility in selecting the proper mates to produce puppies.

HEALTH CONCERNS

All breeds of dogs have genetic problems that must be paid attention to, and just because a male and female do not have evidence of problems does not mean their pedigrees are free of something that might be entirely incapacitating. Again, rely upon recommendations from national kennel clubs or local breed clubs when looking for a breeder.

Like most other breeds, the Alaskan Malamute is subject to hip dysplasia and cataracts. The breed has a problem of its own called chondrodysplasia, or in layman's terms, *dwarfism.*

Chondroydysplasia is hereditary and devastating to loving owners. The condition is detectable by x-ray. It becomes increasingly observable as the puppy grows and his legs become deformed. This hereditary disease is the result of a simple recessive gene (both sire and dam must carry the gene) that can be carried by non-afflicted dogs. Therefore, responsible breeders work with test-bred stock and are very much aware of where it does and does not exist in some lines.

Hobby breeders will just as easily be included on the recommended lists obtained from kennel clubs as names of people who maintain many dogs. These hobby breeders are equally dedicated to producing quality Alaskan Malamutes and in many cases have even more opportunity to devote to the all-important socialization process. They also will be able to give an expert evaluation of the temperament of each puppy, as they have lived with the litter since birth.

Some people will want a more docile Malamute while others want a rough-and-tumble dog that will want to climb mountains and swim rivers with them. Someone who has watched each puppy in the litter grow will be able to advise you in this respect. Be aware, however—the most mild-mannered Malamute is never going to act like a Basset Hound. Malamutes are *all dog!*

Again, it is important that both the buyer and the seller ask questions. We would be highly suspicious of a person who is willing to sell you an Alaskan Malamute puppy "no questions asked."

RECOGNIZING A HEALTHY PUPPY

Most breeders do not release their puppies until they have been given their "puppy shots." Normally, this is at about seven to eight weeks of age. By this time, the litter is entirely weaned. Nursing puppies receive their immunizations from their mother. Once weaned, however, a puppy is highly susceptible to many infectious diseases that can be transmitted via the hands and clothing of people. Therefore, it behooves you to make sure your puppy is fully inoculated before he leaves his home environment and when any additional inoculations should be given.

It is important that your Malamute has time to socialize with his littermates in order to learn how to interact with other dogs later in life. Sisters Keeska and Kiana are the best of friends!

Above all, the Malamute puppy you buy should be a happy bouncy extrovert. The worst thing you could possibly do is buy a shy, shrinking violet puppy or one that appears sick and listless

because you feel sorry for him. Doing this will undoubtedly lead to heartache and difficulty—to say nothing of the veterinary costs that you may incur in getting the puppy well.

If at all possible, take the puppy you are interested in away from his littermates into another room or another part of the kennel. The smells will remain the same for the puppy so he should still feel secure and maintain his outgoing personality, but it will give you an opportunity to inspect the puppy more closely. A healthy little Malamute puppy will be strong and sturdy to the touch, never bony or obese and bloated. The inside of the puppy's ears should be pink and clean. Dark discharge or a bad odor could indicate ear mites, sure signs of poor maintenance. The healthy Malamute puppy's breath smells sweet. The teeth are clean and white and there should never be any malformation of the mouth or jaw. The puppy's eyes should be clear, bright and have that little spark so typical of a Malamute baby. Eyes that appear runny and irritated indicate serious problems.

A well-adjusted Alaskan Malamute puppy will enjoy being held and cuddled and should not show fear or shy away from people.

There should be no sign of discharge from the nose, nor should it be crusted or runny. Coughing or diarrhea are danger signals, as are any eruptions on the skin. The coat should be soft and lustrous.

The healthy Malamute puppy's front legs should be straight as little posts, and the movement light and bouncy. The best way to describe an Alaskan Malamute puppy movement is like that of a mechanical wind-up toy with legs that cover considerable ground. Of course there is always a chubby, clumsy puppy or two

A healthy Malamute puppy will look strong and sturdy with straight front legs.

in a litter. Do not mistake this for unsoundness, but if ever you have any doubts, discuss them with the breeder.

MALE OR FEMALE?

There are many breeds in which the sex of a dog makes little difference to the pet owner. We would not say this is so in the case of the Alaskan Malamute. While both the male and the female are capable of becoming excellent companions and are equally easy to housebreak, do consider the fact that a male Malamute will mature to be considerably larger than his female littermates. He will weigh a great deal more and in most cases have considerably more coat to deal with. These are factors which should be taken into consideration, as they require more physical strength and greater maintenance time on the part of the owner.

There are other sex-related differences to consider as well. While the Malamute is one of the cleanest and easiest breeds to housebreak, the male provides a sexually-related problem in that respect. The male of any breed of dog has a natural instinct to lift his leg and "mark" his territory. The amount of effort that is involved in training the male not to do this varies with the individual dog, but what must be remembered is a male considers everything in the household a part of his territory and has an innate urge to establish this fact. This unfortunately may include your designer drapery or newly upholstered sofa.

If you already have a male dog in your household or are thinking of becoming a two-dog family at some point, you should purchase a female. Two Malamutes of the same sex can be a problem. Malamutes are a dominant breed and extremely territorial. Fights can occur and trying to remove a fighting Malamute from the scene can be both difficult and hazardous to your well being.

Females, on the other hand, have their own set of problems. Females have their semi-annual heat cycles once they are over a year of age. During these heat cycles of approximately 21 days, the female must be confined to avoid soiling her surroundings with the bloody discharge that accompanies estrus. She must also be carefully watched to prevent males from gaining access to her or she will become pregnant.

Both of these sexually related problems can be avoided by

having the pet Malamute "altered." Spaying the female and neutering the male saves the pet owner all the headaches of either of the sexually related problems without changing the character of the Malamute. If there is any change at all in the altered Malamute, it is in making the dog an even more amiable companion. Above all, altering your pet precludes the possibility of his adding to the serious pet overpopulation problems that exist world-wide.

SELECTING A SHOW PROSPECT PUPPY

Should you be considering a show career for your puppy, all the foregoing regarding soundness and health apply here as well. It must be remembered though, spaying and castration are not reversible procedures and once done, eliminate the possibility of ever breeding or showing your Malamute in conformation shows. Altered dogs can, however, be

This determined little guy is an excellent example of what one might look for in a show prospect Alaskan Malamute.

shown in obedience trials and agility.

There are a good number of additional points to be considered for the show dog as well. First of all, it should be remembered the most any breeder can offer is an opinion on the "show potential" of a particular puppy. The most promising eight-week-old puppy can grow up to be a mediocre adult.

Any predictions breeders make about a puppy's future are based upon their experience with past litters that have produced winning show dogs. It is obvious the more successful a breeder has been in producing winning Alaskan Malamutes over the years, the broader his or her base of comparison will be.

A puppy's potential as a show dog is determined by how closely it adheres to the demands of the standard of the breed. While most breeders concur there is no such thing as "a sure thing" when it comes to predicting winners, they are also quick to agree the older a puppy is, the better your chances of making any predictions. We have found grading a litter and evaluating the puppies are best done at exactly eight weeks of age.

It makes little difference to the owner of a pet if their Malamute is a bit too small or too large or if an ear hangs down a bit. Neither would it make a difference if a male pup had only one testicle. These faults do not interfere with a Malamute becoming a healthy, loving companion. However these flaws would keep that Malamute from a winning show career.

While it certainly behooves the prospective buyer of a show prospect puppy to be as familiar with the standard of the breed as possible, it is even more important for the buyer to put his or her self into the hands of a successful and respected breeder of winning Malamutes. The experienced breeder knows there are certain age-related shortcomings in a young Alaskan Malamute that maturity will take care of and other faults that will completely eliminate him from consideration as a show prospect. Also, breeders are always looking for the right homes in which to place their show-prospect puppies and will be particularly helpful when they know you plan to show one of their dogs.

The important thing to remember in choosing your first show prospect is "cuteness" may not be consistent with

When selecting a Malamute for show, you must not be swayed by cuteness. Trust the breeder's insight about how each pup will develop.

quality. An extroverted puppy in the litter might decide it belongs to you. If you are simply looking for a pet, that is the Malamute puppy for you. However, if you are genuinely interested in showing your Alaskan Malamute, you must keep your head and, without disregarding good temperament, give serious consideration to what the standard says a show-type Malamute must be.

Who knows how far your Malamute puppy may go? Crystal, here at eight weeks of age, grew up to be an obedience trial star!

Look for the pup in a litter that is sound—both mentally and physically. It must have an outgoing and confident attitude. A Malamute without a feeling of self-importance will seldom develop into an outstanding show dog.

Color is not important in a Malamute show dog. There is an old saying among dog fanciers that to a good degree applies to Malamutes. "A good dog can't be a bad color." There are a myriad of colors and markings in the breed, but markings should be symmetrical. Underbodies, legs, feet and part of the dog's face markings will be white.

Discuss potential coat length with the breeder. There is a coat factor in the breed that produces very long soft, guard hair. This is undesirable for show or breeding purposes, but Malamutes with this coat type make beautiful pets. We always place puppies of this type as pets and make sure they are spayed or neutered. Malamutes with the long coats make perfectly good pets and there are combs and brushes that assist in keeping these coats in good condition. Coats of this type are not correct and would serve as a handicap for a working sled dog in extremely harsh weather conditions.

Any puppy that appears short on his legs or too long in his body should not be considered at all for the show ring. The overall impression is of a little tank—broad and sturdy from one end to the other.

You want a puppy with strong, straight, gun-barrel front legs. A spindly looking pup is all wrong for an Alaskan Malamute. The tail is carried up and curved over the back.

Dark eyes are preferred and they sit obliquely in the skull, giving them a slight "Oriental" look. The nose must be black except in the red-coated dogs with a brown nose. The muzzle is bulky and strong-looking. The ears are small, stiff and erect.

These are the obvious characteristics of a Malamute puppy with show potential. There are many nuances of breed type that are best understood by an experienced breeder of show-quality Alaskan Malamutes. Rely upon someone who has had this experience to assist you in selecting a puppy of promise. There is an old breeder's saying that applies well here: "Breed the best to the best. Select the best and then hope for the best!"

PUPPY OR ADULT?

A young puppy is not your only option when contemplating the purchase of an Alaskan Malamute. In some cases an adult dog may be just the answer. It certainly eliminates the trials and tribulations of housebreaking, chewing and the myriad of other problems associated with a young puppy.

On occasion, adult Malamutes are available from kennels or homes breeding show dogs. Their breeders realize the older Malamute would be far happier in a family situation where he can watch TV, take hikes and be a part of a family instead of living out his life in a kennel run.

Adult Malamutes seem to adjust to their new homes with great enthusiasm. Most new owners are amazed at how quickly it all happens and how quickly these adults become devoted to their new families!

An adult Alaskan Malamute which comes from a kind and loving environment could be the perfect answer for the elderly or someone who is forced to be away from home during the day. While it would be unreasonable to expect a young puppy not to relieve himself in the house if you are gone many hours, it would be surprising to find a Malamute who in adulthood would even consider relieving himself in the home in which he lives.

A few adult Malamutes may have become set in their ways and while you may not have to contend with the problems of puppyhood, do realize there is the rare adult that might have developed habits which do not entirely suit you or your lifestyle. Arrange to bring an adult Malamute into your home on a trial basis. That way neither you nor the dog will be obligated should either of you decide you are incompatible.

IDENTIFICATION PAPERS

The purchase of any purebred dog entitles you to three very important documents: a health record containing an inoculation list, a copy of the dog's pedigree and the registration certificate.

Health Record

Most Malamute breeders have initiated the necessary inoculation series for their puppies by the time they are eight weeks of age. These inoculations protect the puppies against hepatitis, leptospirosis, distemper and canine parvovirus. In most cases, rabies inoculations are not given until a puppy is four months of age or older.

A mature Tote-Um Kennels male Malamute in full winter coat.
There is a set series of inoculations developed to combat these infectious diseases, and it is extremely important that you obtain a record of the shots your puppy has been given and the dates upon

which the shots were administered. In this way, the veterinarian you choose will be able to continue on with the appropriate inoculation series as needed.

Pedigree

The pedigree is your dog's "family tree." The breeder must supply you with a copy of this document authenticating your puppy's ancestors back to at least the third generation. All purebred dogs have a pedigree. The pedigree does not imply that a dog is of show quality. It is simply a chronological list of ancestors.

Registration Certificate

The registration certificate is the canine world's "birth certificate." This certificate is issued by a country's governing kennel club. When you transfer the ownership of your Malamute from the breeder's name to your own name, the transaction is entered on this certificate and, once mailed to the kennel club, it is permanently recorded in their computerized files. Keep all these documents in a safe place as you will need them when

The puppy you buy will be a member of your family for a long time, so be sure to obtain the healthiest youngster available. Tikaani is pictured at twelve years of age.

Reputable breeders will have started your Malamute puppy on the road to good nutrition so stick to this original diet and make any changes gradual.

you visit your veterinarian or should you ever wish to breed or show your Malamute.

DIET SHEET

Your Alaskan Malamute is the happy healthy puppy he is because the breeder has been carefully feeding and caring for him. Every breeder we know has their own particular way of doing this. Most breeders give the new owner a written record that details the amount and kind of food a puppy has been receiving. Do follow these recommendations to the letter at least for the first month or two after the puppy comes to live with you.

The diet sheet should indicate the number of times a day your puppy has been accustomed to being fed and the kind of vitamin supplementation, if any, he has been receiving. Following the prescribed procedure will reduce the chance of upset stomach and loose stools.

Alaskan Malamute puppies grow very fast. We feed and recommend a high-quality puppy kibble and add raw meat to the diet at about three months. We change to an adult kibble somewhere between six and nine months and continue to add meat.

Usually a breeder's diet sheet projects the increases and

changes in food that will be necessary as your puppy grows from week to week. If the sheet does not include this information, ask the breeder for suggestions regarding increases and the eventual changeover to adult food.

In the unlikely event you are not supplied with a diet sheet by the breeder and are unable to get one, your veterinarian will be able to advise you in this respect. There are countless foods now being manufactured expressly to meet the nutritional needs of puppies and growing dogs. A trip down the pet aisle at your supermarket or pet supply store will prove just how many choices you have. Two important tips to remember: read labels carefully for content, and if you deal with established, reliable manufacturers, you are more likely to get what you pay for.

Alaskan Malamutes are happiest when they get plenty of exercise. Five-month-old Rebel looks energized after a ten-mile hike.

HEALTH GUARANTEE

Any reputable breeder is more than willing to supply a written agreement that the sale of your Malamute is contingent upon his passing a veterinarian's examination. Ideally you will be able to arrange an appointment with your chosen veterinarian right after you have picked up your puppy from the breeder and before you take the puppy home. If this is not possible, you should not delay this procedure any longer than 24 hours from the time you take your puppy home.

TEMPERAMENT AND SOCIALIZATION

Temperament is both hereditary and learned. Inherited good temperament can be ruined by poor treatment and lack of proper socialization. A Malamute puppy that has inherited a bad temperament is a poor risk as either a companion or show dog and should certainly never be bred. Therefore it is critical

Mary Jane Holabach proudly displays a three-week-old Williwaw puppy.

that you obtain a happy puppy from a breeder who is determined to produce good temperaments and has taken all the necessary steps to provide the early socialization necessary.

Temperaments in the same litter can range from strong-willed and outgoing on the high end of the scale to reserved and retiring at the low end. A puppy that is so bold and strong-willed as to be foolhardy and uncontrollable could easily be a difficult adult that needs a very firm hand. This is hardly a dog for the owner who is mild and reserved in demeanor or frail in physique. In every human-canine relationship there must be a pack leader and a follower. The Malamute, which is historically dominant in character, must have an owner who remains in charge at all times or the dog will attempt to assume command.

It is important to remember a Malamute puppy may be as happy as a clam living at home with you and your family, but if the socialization begun by the breeder is not continued, that sunny disposition will not extend outside your front door. From the day the young Malamute arrives at your home you must be committed to accompanying him upon an unending pilgrimage to meet and like all human beings and animals.

If you are fortunate enough to have children well past the toddler stage in the household or living nearby, your socialization task will be assisted considerably. Malamutes raised with children are the best. The two seem to understand each other and in some way known only to the puppies and children themselves, they give each other the confidence to face the trying ordeal of growing up.

The children in your own household are not the only children your puppy should spend time with. It is a case of the more the merrier! Every child (and adult for that matter) that enters your household should be asked to pet your puppy.

Your puppy should go everywhere with you: the post office, the market, the shopping mall—wherever. Be prepared to create a stir wherever you go because the very qualities that attracted you to the first Malamute you met applies here as well. Everyone will want to pet your little "teddy bear" and there is nothing in the world better for him.

Should your puppy back off from a stranger, give the person a treat to offer your puppy. You must insist your young Malamute be amenable to the attention of all strangers—young and old, short and tall, and of all races. It is not up to your puppy to decide who it will or will not be friendly with. You are in charge. You must call the shots.

Socialize your Alaskan Malamute with people and other pets. A well-socialized puppy will get along with anybody or anything!

If your Alaskan Malamute has a show career in his future, there are other things in addition to just being handled that will have to be taught. All show dogs must learn to have their mouths opened and inspected by the judge. The judge must be able to check the teeth. Males must be accustomed to having their testicles touched, as the dog show judge must determine that all male dogs are "complete," that means there are two normal-sized testicles in the scrotum. These inspections must begin in puppyhood and be done on a regular and continuing basis.

Temperaments in the same litter can range from strong-willed to reserved. Choose the pup that best suits your personality.

All Malamutes must learn to get on with other dogs as well as with humans. If you are fortunate enough to have a dog training class nearby, attend with as much regularity as you possibly can. A young Malamute that has been regularly exposed to other dogs from puppyhood will learn to adapt and accept other dogs and other breeds much more readily than one that seldom sees strange dogs.

THE ADOLESCENT MALAMUTE

You will find it amazing how quickly the little ball of fur you first brought home begins to develop into a full-grown Alaskan Malamute. Some lines shoot up to full size very rapidly, others mature more slowly. A few Malamutes pass through adolescence quite gracefully, but at about nine months, most become lanky and ungainly growing in and out of proportion seemingly from one day to the next.

Somewhere between 12 to 18 months, your Malamute will have attained its full height. However, body and coat development continue on until two years of age in some lines and up to three or four years of age in others. Food needs increase during this growth period and some dogs seem as if they can never get enough to eat. Think of puppies as individualistic as children and act accordingly.

The amount of food you give your Malamute puppy should

be adjusted to how much it will readily consume at each meal. If the food is eaten too quickly, add a small amount with the next feeding and continue to do so as need increases. This method will insure you of giving your dog enough food, but you must also pay close attention to the dog's appearance and condition, as you do not want your dog to become overweight or obese.

At eight weeks of age a Malamute puppy is eating two to three meals a day. By the time it is six months old, a Malamute can do well on two meals a day. If your dog does not eat the food offered, it is either not hungry or not well. Your dog will eat when it is hungry. If you suspect the dog is not well, a trip to the veterinarian is in order.

All Malamutes pass through a period when the puppy coat is shed and the adult coat is beginning to come in. It is essential you give grooming all the attention it requires at this time to remove the dead puppy hair so the new coat can come through easily.

The Malamute's "terrible teens" may also bring out a "testing" personality. The puppy wants to see just how far it can go. It is extremely important to be firm and let the puppy know it is you who are in charge!

This adolescent period is a particularly important one as it is the time your Malamute must learn all the household and social rules by which he will live for the rest of his life. Your patience and commitment during this time not only will produce a respected canine good citizen but will forge a bond between the two of you that will grow and ripen into a wonderful relationship.

THE MALAMUTE PROTECTION LEAGUE

There is a national rescue service for Alaskan Malamutes that all those who love the

Like all puppies, young Malamutes are notorious chewers. Make sure your dog's chew toys are safe and can't break apart and be swallowed.

Your Malamute puppy will probably test your authority by seeing how much he can get away with. Four-month-old Ivaloo looks ready, willing and able to get into trouble!

breed should be aware of. This is the Alaskan Malamute Protection League (AMPL). It is comprised of people who care about all Malamutes and have organized an information network, clearing house and emergency funding service.

The AMPL rescues Malamutes from pounds, shelters and abandonment situations They also intervene in "puppy mill" seizures and other situations that put Malamutes at risk.

People who have the time, patience and communication skills volunteer their services as state coordinators. There are those who temporarily house misplaced Malamutes and still others who provide transportation of rehomed Malamutes.

All of this work is done by volunteers and continues through the generosity of friends and owners of the breed. Anyone wishing additional information may obtain it by contacting the Alaskan Malamute Club of America.

CARING for Your Alaskan Malamute

The best way to make sure your Malamute puppy is obtaining the right amount and the correct type of food for his age is to follow the diet sheet provided by the breeder from whom you obtained your puppy. Do your best not to change the puppy's diet and you will be less apt to run into digestive problems and diarrhea. Diarrhea is very serious in young puppies. Puppies with diarrhea can dehydrate very rapidly, causing severe problems and even death.

If it is necessary to change your puppy's diet for any reason, it should be done gradually, over a period of several meals and a few days. Begin by adding a tablespoon or two of the new food, gradually increasing the amount until the meal consists entirely of the new product.

By the time your Malamute puppy is 12 months old, you can reduce feedings to one a day. This meal can be given either in the morning or evening. It is really a matter of choice on your part. There are two important things to remember: Feed the main meal at the same time every day and make sure what you feed is nutritionally complete.

If you wish, the single meal can be cut in half and fed twice a day. A morning or night-time snack of hard dog biscuits made

Make clean water available to your Alaskan Malamute puppy at all times.

56

especially for large dogs can also be given. These biscuits not only become highly anticipated treats by your Malamute but are genuinely helpful in maintaining healthy gums and teeth.

"BALANCED" DIETS

In order for a canine diet to qualify as "complete and balanced" in the United States, it must meet standards set by the Subcommittee on Canine Nutrition of the National

Your Malamute puppy's food intake needs to be increased during his growth periods. Each puppy is an individual, however, so adjust his diet accordingly.

Malamutes play hard so be cautious about your dog's health in hot weather. Make him take breaks and be sure he always has cool clean water to drink.

Research Council of the National Academy of Sciences. Most commercial foods manufactured for dogs meet these standards and prove this by listing the ingredients contained in the food on every package and can. The ingredients

If you offer your Alaskan Malamute his food at the same time every day, he will adjust to a regular feeding schedule.

are listed in descending order with the main ingredient listed first.

Fed with any regularity at all, refined sugars can cause your Malamute to become obese and will definitely create tooth decay. Candy stores do not exist in the wild and canine teeth are not genetically disposed to handling sugars. Do not feed your Alaskan Malamute sugar products and avoid products that contain sugar to any high degree.

Fresh water and a properly prepared, balanced diet containing the essential nutrients in correct proportions are all a healthy Malamute needs to be offered. Dog foods come canned, dry, semi-moist, "scientifically fortified" and "all-natural." A visit to your local supermarket or pet store will reveal how vast an array you have to select from.

The important thing to remember is that all dogs, whether they are Malamutes or Chihuahuas, are carnivorous (meat-eating) animals. While the vegetable content of your Malamute's diet should not be overlooked, a dog's physiology and anatomy are based upon carnivorous food acquisition. Protein and fat are absolutely essential to the well-being of your Malamute. In fact, it is wise to add a tablespoon or two of vegetable oil or bacon drippings to your dog's diet, particularly during winter months.

Read the list of ingredients on the dog food you buy. Animal protein should appear first on the label's list of ingredients. A base of quality kibble to which the meat and even table scraps has been added can provide a nutritious meal for your Malamute.

Choose a good-quality dog food for your Alaskan Malamute based on the nutritional requirements for his specific stage of life and activity level.

This having been said, it should be realized in the wild carnivores eat the entire beast they capture and kill. The carnivore's kills consist almost entirely of herbivorous (plant-eating) animals, and invariably the carnivore begins his meal with the contents of the herbivore's stomach. This provides the carbohydrates, minerals and nutrients present in vegetables.

Through centuries of domestication we have made our dogs entirely dependent upon us for their well being. Therefore we are entirely responsible for duplicating the food balance the wild dog finds in nature. The domesticated dog's diet must include protein, carbohydrates, fats, roughage and small amounts of essential minerals and vitamins.

Finding commercially prepared diets that contain all the necessary nutrients will not present a problem. It is important to understand, though, that these commercially prepared foods do contain all the necessary nutrients your Malamute needs. It is therefore unnecessary to add vitamin supplements to these diets in other than special circumstances prescribed by your veterinarian. Over-supplementation and forced growth are now looked upon by some breeders as major contributors to many skeletal abnormalities found in the purebred dogs of the day.

Over Supplementation

A great deal of controversy exists today regarding the orthopedic problems such as hip, elbow and patella (knee) dysplasia that afflict Malamutes and many other breeds. Some claim these problems are entirely hereditary conditions, but many others feel they can be exacerbated by diet and over-use of mineral and vitamin supplements for puppies.

In giving vitamin supplementation one should *never* exceed the prescribed amount. Some breeders insist all recommended dosages be halved before including them in a dog's diet. Still other breeders feel no supplementation should be given at all, believing a balanced diet that includes plenty of milk products and a small amount of bone meal to provide calcium is all that is necessary and beneficial.

Pregnant and lactating bitches may require supplementation of some kind, but here again it is not a case of "if a little is good, a lot would be a great deal better." Extreme caution is advised in this case and best discussed with your veterinarian.

If the owner of an Alaskan Malamute normally eats healthy, nutritious food, there is no reason why their dog can not be given table scraps. What could possibly be harmful in good nutritious food?

Table scraps should be given only as part of the dog's meal and never from the table. A Malamute who becomes accustomed to being hand-fed from the table can become a real pest at mealtime very quickly. Also, dinner guests may find the pleading stare of your Malamute less than appealing when dinner is being served.

Dogs do not care if food looks like a hot dog or wedge of cheese. Truly nutritious dog foods are seldom manufactured to look like food that appeals to humans. Dogs only care about how food smells and tastes. It is highly doubtful you will be eating your dog's food, so do not waste your money on these "looks just like" products.

Along these lines, most of the moist foods or canned foods that have the look of "delicious red beef" look that way because they contain great amounts of preservatives and dyes. Preservatives and dyes are no better for your dog than they are for you.

Special Diets

There are now any number of commercially prepared diets for dogs with special dietary needs. The overweight, underweight or geriatric dog can have its nutritional needs met, as can puppies and growing dogs. The calorie content of these foods is adjusted accordingly. With the correct amount of the right foods and the proper amount of exercise, your Malamute should stay in top shape. Common sense must prevail. What works for humans works for

If you choose to give your Malamute treats, make sure they are nutritious and do not upset his regular meals.

dogs as well—increasing calories will increase weight; stepping up exercise and reducing calories will bring weight down.

Occasionally a young Malamute going through the teething period will become a poor eater. The concerned owner's first response is to tempt the dog by hand-feeding special treats and foods that the problem eater seems to prefer. This practice only serves to compound the problem. Once the dog learns to play the waiting game, he will turn up his nose at anything other than its favorite food knowing full well what it *wants* to eat will eventually arrive.

Dogs have no suicidal tendencies. A healthy dog will not

starve himself to death. He may not eat enough to keep him in the shape we find ideal and attractive, but he will definitely eat enough to maintain himself. If your Malamute is not eating properly and appears to be too thin, it is probably best to consult your veterinarian

BATHING AND GROOMING

It is important to remember the Alaskan Malamute is a natural breed that requires no clipping or trimming outside of tidying up his feet or perhaps removing the whiskers. Breeders are most adamant that the Malamute not fall into any grooming fads of any kind. Proper brushing and a few snips of the scissors around the feet are all the grooming that your Malamute will ever need.

Puppy Coat

Undoubtedly the breeder from whom you purchased your Malamute will have begun to accustom the puppy to grooming just as soon as there was enough hair to brush. We begin doing so at three weeks of age.

If you accustom your Malamute to grooming procedures when he is young, it will become a pleasurable experience for both of you.

Because they shed so heavily and have such a dense undercoat, it is very important that your Malamute be taught to stand for brushing.

You must continue on with grooming sessions or begin them at once if for some reason they have not been started. You and your Malamute will spend a significant amount of time involved with this activity over a lifetime, so it is imperative you both learn to cooperate in the endeavor to make it an easy and pleasant experience.

The easiest way to groom a Malamute is by placing him on a grooming table. A grooming table can be built or purchased at your local pet emporium. Make sure the table is of a height at which you can work comfortably either sitting or standing. Adjustable-height grooming tables are available at most pet shops.

Although you will buy this when your Malamute puppy first arrives, anticipate your dog's full-grown size in making your purchase and select or build a table that will accommodate a fully grown Malamute. We use a grooming table that has an "arm" and a "noose." The noose slips around the dog's neck when it is standing and keeps the dog from fidgeting about or deciding he has had enough grooming and jumping off the table.

You will need to invest in a good brush. We highly recommend one that has a good stiff boar bristle. You will also need a steel comb to remove any debris that collects in the longer furnishings. Consider the fact you will be using this equipment for many years so buy the best of these items that you can afford.

Any attempt to groom your puppy on the floor may result with you spending a good part of your time chasing him around the room. Nor is sitting on the floor for long stretches of time the most comfortable position in the world for the average adult.

When brushing, go through the coat in both directions. Do this all over the body and be especially careful to attend to the hard-to-reach areas. Mats can occur rapidly during the time when the long-coated Malamute is shedding his puppy coat.

Good grooming practices will improve the overall health and well being of your Alaskan Malamute.

Mats will only occur in the long coats. The correct coats never mat.

Should you encounter a mat that does not brush out easily, use your fingers and the steel comb to separate the hairs as much as possible. Do not cut or pull out the matted hair. Apply baby powder or one of the especially prepared grooming powders directly to the mat and brush completely from the skin out.

Nail Trimming

This is a good time to accustom your Malamute to having his nails trimmed and having his feet inspected. Always inspect your dog's feet for cracked pads. Check between the toes for splinters and thorns. Pay particular attention to any swollen or tender areas. In many sections of the country there is a weed

Inspect your Alaskan Malamute's feet for cracked pads, thorns or splinters and trim his nails on a regular basis.

that has a barbed, hook-like projection that carries its seed. This hook can easily find its way into a Malamute's foot or between his toes and very quickly works its way deep into the dog's flesh. This will cause soreness and infection. These barbs are best removed by your veterinarian before serious problems result.

The nails of a Malamute who spends most of his time indoors or on grass when outdoors can grow long very quickly. Do not allow the nails to become overgrown and then expect to cut them back easily. Each nail has a blood vessel running through the center called the "quick." The quick grows close to the end of the nail and contains very sensitive nerve endings. If the nail is allowed to grow too long it will be impossible to cut it back to a proper length without cutting into the quick. This causes severe pain to the dog and can also result in a great deal of bleeding that can be very difficult to stop. We attend to our dog's nails every other week.

If your Malamute is getting plenty of exercise on cement or rough, hard pavement, the nails may keep sufficiently worn down. Otherwise the nails can grow long very quickly. They must then be trimmed with canine nail clippers, an electric nail grinder (also called a drummel) or a coarse file made expressly for that purpose.

The Malamute's dark nails make it practically impossible to see where the quick ends, so regardless of which nail trimming device is used, one must proceed with caution and remove only a small portion of the nail at a time.

Should the quick be nipped in the trimming process, there are any number of blood-clotting products available at pet shops that will almost immediately stem the flow of blood. It is wise to have one of these products on hand in case there is a nail-trimming accident or the dog tears a nail on his own.

An early introduction to water will make bathing your Malamute much easier. Kaila and Apache love their baby pool!

Grooming the Adult Malamute

Fortunately, you and your Malamute have spent the many months between puppyhood and full maturity learning to assist each other through the grooming process. The two of you have survived the shedding of the puppy coat and the arrival of the entirely different adult hair. Not only is the Malamute's adult hair of a much different texture, it is longer and much thicker.

Keep your Alaskan Malamute's ears clean and free of dirt and waxy build-up.

Bathing

We always recommend bathing at shedding time as it helps remove the old coat. Otherwise, following the foregoing coat care procedure will all but eliminate the need for bathing a Malamute more than once or twice a year. Dog show exhibitors use coat-care products that adhere to the Malamute's hair and most exhibitors bathe their Malamutes before shows. Even at that, some Malamute exhibitors do use "dry bath" products rather than the tub and shampoo method. Well-kept Malamutes are literally odor-free and frequent bathing is unnecessary.

On the occasion your Malamute requires a wet bath, you will need to gather the necessary equipment ahead of time. A rubber mat should be placed at the bottom of the tub so your dog can avoid slipping and thereby becoming frightened. A rubber spray hose is absolutely necessary to thoroughly wet the Malamute's dense coat. The hose is also necessary to remove all shampoo residue.

A small cotton ball placed inside each ear will avoid water running down into the dog's ear canal. Be very careful when washing around the eyes as soaps and shampoos can be extremely irritating.

It is best to use a shampoo designed especially for dogs. The Ph balance is adjusted to keep drying to a minimum and leaves the hair shining and lustrous.

In bathing, start behind the ears and work back. Use a wash cloth to soap and rinse around the head and face. Once you have shampooed your dog, you must rinse the coat thoroughly, and when you feel quite certain all shampoo residue has been removed, rinse once more. Shampoo residue in the coat is sure to dry the hair and could cause skin irritation.

As soon as you have completed the bath, use heavy towels to remove as much of the excess water as possible. Your Malamute will assist you in the process by shaking a great deal of the water out of his coat on his own.

Before your Malamute is completely dry it is best to brush out the coat. Use the same brushing process you normally use.

The Malamute was bred for work and loves to use his innate talents. There is nothing they like better than a romp in the snow! Shilon Bedford's team of Malamutes pulls a sled in Wisconsin.

EXERCISE

The Alaskan Malamute is a breed that requires space and loves the opportunity to exercise. Remember the breed's heritage. The Malamute was bred to work!

Needless to say, puppies should never be forced to exercise. Normally, they are little dynamos of energy and keep themselves busy all day long with frequent naps in between their activities. Adults do fine in a large fenced yard.

The adult Malamute does love a long on-leash brisk walk. Of course, this can do nothing but benefit the Malamute's owner as well.

It goes without saying that a romp in the snow is sheer heaven to a Malamute! A trip to the mountains or to the north country could provide a day of sheer bliss for your friend.

Malamutes make great jogging companions.

Puppies are full of boundless energy but should never be forced to exercise or overworked. Crystal takes a much deserved snooze.

SOCIALIZATION

Unlike a good number of other breeds, the Alaskan Malamute is not a needy or dependent dog. The breed is incredibly independent and as long as the person or persons he loves are nearby, the Malamute is completely happy.

On the surface this might appear to be just fine but as the saying goes, "No man (or dog!) is an island." In today's urban society, human and canine must be able to get along with their neighbors. It is up to you to insist, through proper training, that your Malamute understands and adapts to this social rule.

The Alaskan Malamute is a big and powerful dog with a mind of his own. Properly trained, the breed is one of the best canine citizens known to man. The untrained Malamute, on the other hand, is not just a nuisance, he can be a danger to

Parka is in Malamute heaven as she relaxes in her natural habitat.

As long as they are well-socialized and properly introduced, the Alaskan Malamute gets along well with other dogs. Teller, Brook and Tobe share the same house peacefully.

himself and all other creatures he comes in contact with.

Should you wish to have a two-dog household, some careful thought ahead of time can avoid problems. First, it is easier to bring a Malamute puppy into a mature dog's household, especially if the older dog is of the opposite sex and of an amiable disposition. An adult Malamute may not be particularly thrilled to have its home turf invaded by a puppy and might be rough in showing his displeasure if not properly supervised.

Regardless of age, some thought should be given to compatibility. When the choice can be made, it would be wise to choose one of the more passive breeds to share a Malamute's household. Bringing in another breed of the same sex with as dominant a personality as the Malamute's may only lead to problems.

HOUSEBREAKING and Training Your Alaskan Malamute

There is no breed of dog that cannot be trained. It does appear some breeds are more difficult to get the desired response from than others. In many cases however, this has more to do with the trainer and his or her training methods than with the dog's inability to learn. With the proper approach any dog that is not mentally deficient can be taught to be a good canine citizen. Many dog owners do not understand how a dog learns nor do they realize they can be breed specific in their approach to training.

Young puppies have an amazing capacity to learn. This capacity is greater than most humans realize. It is important to remember, though, that these young puppies also forget with great speed

If you begin training your Alaskan Malamute early he will grow to become a valued member of your family.

unless they are reminded of what they have learned by continual reinforcement.

As puppies leave the nest they began their search for two things; a pack leader and the rules set down by that leader by which the puppies can abide. Because puppies, particularly Alaskan Malamute puppies, are cuddly and cute, some owners fail miserably in supplying these very basic needs of every dog.

Instead the owner immediately begins to respond to the demands of the puppy and Malamute puppies can quickly learn to be very demanding.

For example, a Malamute puppy quickly learns he will be allowed into the house because he is whining, not because he can only enter the house when he is *not* whining. Instead of learning the only way he will be fed is to follow a set procedure (i.e., sitting or lying down on command), the Malamute puppy learns leaping about the kitchen and creating a stir are what gets results.

Dogs learn the rules of dogdom from their dam and littermates, but it is up to you, the owner, to teach your Malamute the rules he must follow.

If the young puppy cannot find his pack leader in an owner, the puppy assumes the role of pack leader. If there are no rules imposed, the puppy learns to make his own rules. And, unfortunately, the negligent owner continually reinforces the puppy's decisions by allowing him to govern the household.

With small dogs this scenario can produce a neurotic nuisance. In a top-size dog like the Malamute, the situation can be downright dangerous. Neither situation is an acceptable one.

The key to successful training lies in establishing the proper relationship between dog and owner. The owner or the owning family must be the pack leader and the individual or family must provide the rules by which the dog abides.

Once leadership is established, ease of training depends in great part upon just how much a dog depends upon his master's approval. The entirely dependent dog lives to please his master and will do everything in his power to evoke the approval response from the person to whom he is devoted.

At the opposite end of the pole, we have the totally independent dog who is not remotely concerned with what his master thinks. Dependency varies from one breed to the next and to a degree within breeds as well. Malamutes are no exception to this rule.

Housebreaking

After the long preceding discourse on the independent nature of the Malamute, let us say the breed is at the same time extremely clean and extremely easy to housebreak. Perhaps this is because the Malamute wants to be clean; whatever the reason, many Malamute puppies are housebroken in matter of days rather than of weeks or months as is the case in a good number of other breeds.

Consistency

The method of housebreaking we recommend is the avoidance of accidents happening. We take a puppy outdoors to relieve itself after every meal, after every nap and after every 15 or 20 minutes of playtime. We carry the puppy outdoors to avoid the opportunity of an accident occurring on the way.

The Crate Method: First-time dog owners are inclined to initially see the crate method of housebreaking as cruel. What they do not understand is that all dogs, particularly the Malamute, need a place of their own to retreat to, and you will find the Malamute will consider his crate that place.

Use of a crate reduces housetraining time to an absolute minimum and avoids keeping a puppy under constant stress by incessantly correcting him for making mistakes in the house. The anti-crate advocates who consider it cruel to confine a

Your Alaskan Malamute will crave the security of his own "den." A crate will provide your dog with unlimited access to his own private space.

puppy for any length of time do not seem to have a problem with constantly harassing and punishing the puppy because he has wet on the carpet and relieved himself behind the sofa.

The crate used for housebreaking should only be large enough for the puppy to stand up and lie down in and stretch out comfortably. It is not necessary to dash out and buy a new crate every few weeks to accommodate the Malamute's

Crate training is the quickest and easier way to housebreak your Alaskan Malamute puppy.

rapid spurts of growth. Simply cut a piece of plywood of a size to partition off the excess space in the very large cage and move it back as needed. Long before you have lost the need for the partition your Malamute will be housebroken.

Begin using the crate to feed your Malamute puppy. Keep the door closed and latched while the puppy is eating. When the meal is finished, open the cage and carry the puppy outdoors to the spot where you want him to learn to eliminate. In the event you do not have outdoor access or will be away from home for long periods of time, begin housebreaking by placing newspapers in some out-of-the-way corner that is easily accessible for the puppy. If you consistently take your puppy to the same spot, you will reinforce the habit of going there for that purpose.

It is important that you do not let the puppy loose after eating. Young puppies will eliminate almost immediately after eating or drinking. They will also be ready to relieve themselves when they first wake up and after playing. If you keep a watchful eye on your puppy, you will quickly learn when this is about to take place. A puppy usually circles and sniffs the floor just before relieving himself. Do not give your puppy an opportunity to learn that he can eliminate in the house! Your housetraining chores will be reduced considerably if you avoid bad habits in the first place.

If you are not able to watch your puppy every minute, he should be in his cage or crate with the door securely latched. Each time you put your puppy in the crate, give him a small treat of some kind. Throw the treat to the back of the cage and encourage the puppy to walk in on his own. When he does so, praise the puppy and perhaps hand him another piece of the treat through the wires of the cage.

Do not succumb to your puppy's complaints about being in his crate. The puppy must learn to stay there and to do so without unnecessary complaining. A quick "no" command and a tap on the crate will usually get the puppy to understand theatrics will not result in liberation.

Do understand a puppy of eight to twelve weeks will not be able to contain himself for long periods of time. Puppies of that age must relieve themselves often, except at night. Your schedule must be adjusted accordingly. Also make sure your puppy has relieved himself of both bowel and bladder the last thing at night.

Your first priority in the morning is to get the puppy outdoors. Just how early this ritual will take place will depend much more upon your puppy than upon you. If your Malamute is like most others, there will be no doubt in your mind when he needs to be let out. You will also very quickly learn to tell the difference between the "this is an emergency" complaint and the "I just want out" grumbling. Do not test the young puppy's ability to contain himself. His vocal demand to be let out is confirmation that the housebreaking lesson is being learned.

Should you find it necessary to be away from home all day, you will not be able to leave your puppy in a crate; but on the other hand, do not make the mistake of allowing him to roam the house or even a large room at will. Confine the puppy to a small room or partitioned-off area and cover the floor with newspaper. Make this area large enough so that the puppy will not have to relieve himself next to his bed, food or water bowls. You will soon find the puppy will be inclined to use one particular spot to perform his bowel and bladder functions. When you are home you must take the puppy to this exact spot to eliminate at the appropriate time.

Basic Training

Where you are emotionally and the environment in which you train are just as important to your dog's training as his state of mind at the time. Never begin training when you are irritated, distressed or preoccupied. Nor should you begin basic training in a place that interferes with you or your dog's concentration. Once the commands are understood and learned, you can begin testing your dog in public places, but at first the two of you should work in a place where you can concentrate fully upon each other.

The "No" Command

There is no doubt whatsoever one of the most important commands your Malamute puppy will ever learn is the meaning of the "no" command. It is critical that the puppy learn this command just as soon as possible. One important piece of advice in using this and all other commands—*never give a command you are not prepared and able to enforce!* The only way a puppy learns to obey commands is to realize that once issued, commands must be complied with. Learning the "no" command should start on the first day of the puppy's arrival at your home.

For safety reasons, make sure your Alaskan Malamute wears his collar and identification tags.

Leash Training

It is never too early to accustom the Malamute puppy to a collar and leash. It is your way of keeping your dog under control. It may not be necessary for the puppy or adult Malamute to wear his collar and identification tags within the confines of your home, but no Malamute should ever leave home without a collar and without the leash held securely in your hand.

Begin getting your Malamute puppy accustomed to his collar by leaving it on for a few minutes at a time. Gradually extend the time you leave the collar on. Most Malamute puppies become accustomed to their collar very quickly and forget they are even wearing one. We start with a buckle collar on young puppies.

Once this is accomplished, attach a lightweight leash to the collar while you are playing with the puppy. Do not try to

Because there are a lot of distractions in the great outdoors, your Alaskan Malamute should always be on lead when walking outside.

guide the puppy at first. The point here is to accustom the puppy to the feeling of having something attached to the collar.

Encourage your puppy to follow you as you move away. Should the puppy be reluctant to cooperate, coax him along with a treat of some kind. Hold the treat in front of the puppy's nose to encourage him to follow you. Just as soon as the puppy takes a few steps toward you, praise him enthusiastically and continue to do so as you continue to move along.

Make the initial session very brief and very enjoyable. Continue the lessons in your home or yard until the puppy is completely unconcerned about the fact that he is on a leash. With a treat in one hand and the leash in the other, you can begin to use both to guide the puppy in the direction you wish to go. Your walks can begin in front of the house and eventually extend down the street and eventually around the block.

The "Come" Command

The next most important lesson for the Malamute puppy to learn is to come when called. Therefore, it is very important that the puppy learn his name as soon as possible. Constant repetition is what does the trick in teaching a puppy his name. Use the name every time you talk to your puppy.

Learning to "come" on command could save your Malamute's life when the two of you venture out into the world. "Come" is the command a dog must understand has to be obeyed without question, but the dog should not associate that command with fear. Your dog's response to his name and the word "come" should always be associated with a pleasant experience such as great praise and petting or a food treat.

It is much easier to avoid the establishment of bad habits than it is to correct them once set. *Never* give the "come" command unless you are sure your Malamute puppy will come to you. The very young puppy is far more inclined to respond to learning the "come" command than the older Malamute. Use the command initially when the puppy is already on his way to you or give the command while walking or running away from the

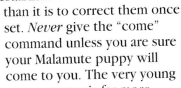

Malamute puppies are innately curious and have a knack for getting into all kinds of trouble. Closely supervise your puppy at all times.

youngster. Clap your hands and sound very happy and excited about having the puppy join in on this "game."

The very young Malamute will normally want to stay as close to his owner as possible, especially in strange surroundings. When your puppy sees you moving away, his natural inclination will be to get close to you. This is a perfect time to use the "come" command.

Later, as the puppy grows more independent and more headstrong (as the young Malamute can do), you may want to attach a long leash or rope to the puppy's collar to ensure the correct response. Do not chase or punish your puppy for not obeying the "come" command. Doing so in the initial stages of training makes the youngster associate the command with something to fear and this will result in avoidance rather than the immediate positive response you desire. It is imperative that you praise your puppy and give him a treat when he does come to you, even if he voluntarily delays responding for many minutes.

Use hand signals in conjunction with verbal commands when training your Malamute. This dog learns the command for "sit."

The "Sit" and "Stay" Commands

Just as important to your Malamute's safety (and your sanity!) as the "no" command and learning to come when called are the "sit" and "stay" commands. Even very young Malamutes can learn the sit command quickly, especially if it appears to be a game and a food treat is involved.

First, remember the Malamute-in-training should always be on collar and leash for all his lessons. A Malamute puppy is not beyond getting up and walking away when he has decided enough is too much!

Give the "sit" command, tug his collar up immediately before gently pushing down on your puppy's hindquarters or scooping his hind legs under the dog, molding him into a sit position. Praise the dog lavishly when he does sit, even though it is you who made the action take place. Again, a food treat always seems to get the lesson across to the learning youngster.

Continue holding the dog's rear end down and repeat the "sit" command several times. If your dog makes an attempt to get up, repeat the command yet again while exerting pressure on the rear end until the correct position is assumed. Make your Malamute stay in this position for increasing lengths of time. Begin with a few seconds and increase the time as lessons progress over the following weeks.

Should your Malamute student attempt to get up or to lie down, he should be corrected by simply saying "sit!" in a firm voice. This should be accompanied by returning the dog to the desired position. Only when you decide your dog should get up should he be allowed to do so. Do not test the young puppy's patience to the limits. Remember you are dealing with a baby and the attention span of any youngster is relatively short.

When you do decide the dog can get up, call his name, say "OK" and make a big fuss over him. Praise and a food treat are in order every time your Malamute responds correctly.

Once your puppy has mastered the "sit" lesson, you may start on the "stay" command. With your dog on leash and facing you, command it to "sit," then take a step or two back. If your dog attempts to get up to follow, firmly say, "Sit, stay!" While you are saying this, raise your hand, palm toward the dog, and again command "Stay!"

Any attempt on your dog's part to get up must be corrected at once, returning him to the sit position and repeating, "Stay!" Once your Malamute begins to understand what you want, you can gradually increase the distance you step back. With a long leash attached to your dog's collar (even a clothesline will do), start with a few steps and gradually increase the distance to several yards. Your Malamute must eventually learn the "Sit, stay" command must be obeyed no matter how far away you are. Later on, with advanced training, your dog will learn the command is to be obeyed even when you move entirely out of sight.

As your Malamute masters this lesson and is able to remain in the sit position for as long as you dictate, avoid calling the dog to you at first. This makes the dog overly anxious to get up and run to you. Instead, walk back to your dog and say "OK," which is a signal that the command is over.

The "sit, stay" lesson can take considerable time and patience especially with the Malamute puppy, whose attention span will be very short. It is best to keep the "stay" part of the lesson to a minimum until the Malamute puppy is five or six months old. Everything in a very young Malamute's makeup urges him to follow you wherever you go. Forcing a very young Malamute to operate against his natural instincts can be bewildering for the puppy.

The "Down" Command

Once your Malamute has mastered the "sit" and "stay" commands, you may begin work on "down." This is the single-word command for lie down. Use the "down" command *only* when you want the dog to lie down. If you want your dog to get off your sofa or to stop jumping up on people, use the "off" command. Do not interchange these two commands. Doing so will only serve to confuse your dog and evoking the right response will become next to impossible.

The "down" position is especially useful if you want your Malamute to remain in a particular place for a period of time. A Malamute is far more inclined to stay put when he is lying down than when he is sitting.

Teaching this command to your Malamute may take more time and patience than the previous lessons the two of you have undertaken. It is believed by some animal behaviorists that assuming the "down" position somehow represents submissiveness to the dog. Considering the highly independent nature and dominant personality of our Malamutes, it is easy to understand how this command could prove more difficult for them to accept. In the end, once the "down" command has become a part of your dog's repertory, it seems to be more relaxing for you and you will find your dog seems less inclined to get up and wander off.

An Alaskan Malamute obeying the "down" command from his owner Raissa Rubenstein.

With your Malamute sitting in front of and facing you, hold a treat in your right hand with the excess part of the leash in your left hand. Hold the treat under the dog's nose and slowly bring your hand down to the ground. Your dog will follow

the treat with its head and neck. As it does, give the command "down" and exert light pressure on the dog's shoulders with your left hand. If your dog resists the pressure on its shoulders, *do not continue pushing down,* doing so will only create more resistance.

An alternative method of getting your Malamute headed into the down position is to move around to the dog's right side and as you draw his attention downward with your right hand, slide your left arm under the dog's front legs and gently slide them forward. In the case of a small puppy, you will undoubtedly have to be on your knees next to the youngster.

As your Malamute's forelegs begin to slide out to his front, keep moving the treat along the ground until the dog's whole body is lying on the ground while you continually repeat "down." Once your Malamute has assumed the position you desire, give it the treat and a lot of praise. Continue assisting your dog into the "down" position until he does so on his own. Be firm and be patient.

The "down" command is a difficult one for your Malamute to accept because it puts him in a submissive position.

The "Heel" Command

In learning to heel, your Malamute will walk on your left side with his shoulder next to your leg no matter which direction you might go or how quickly you turn. Teaching your Malamute to heel will not only make your daily walks far more enjoyable, it will make for a far more tractable companion when the two of you are in crowded or confusing situations. We use a buckle collar on puppies until they are at least four months old. After that age we have found a lightweight, link-chain training collar is very useful for the heeling lesson. It provides both quick pressure around the neck and a snapping sound, both of which get the dog's attention. Erroneously referred to as a "choke collar," the link-chain collar used properly will not choke the dog. The pet

All dogs should learn to walk calmly by your side without pulling. An Alaskan Malamute practicing the "heel" command. shop at which you purchase the training collar will be able to show you the proper way to put this collar on your dog. Do not leave this collar on your puppy when training sessions are finished as it may damage his thick coat.

As you train your puppy to walk along on the leash, you should accustom the youngster to walk on your left side. The leash should cross your body from the dog's collar to your right hand. The excess portion of the leash will be folded into your right hand and your left hand on the leash will be used to make corrections with the leash.

A quick, short jerk on the leash with your left hand will keep your dog from lunging side to side, pulling ahead or lagging back. As you make a correction, give the "heel"

Positive reinforcement, praise and affection are the best training motivators for your Alaskan Malamute.

command. Always keep the leash slack as long as your dog maintains the proper position at your side.

If your dog begins to drift away, give the leash a sharp jerk and guide the dog back to the correct position and give the "heel" command. Do not pull on the lead with steady pressure. What is needed is a sharp but gentle jerking motion and a treat to get your dog's attention.

Training Classes

There are few limits to what a patient, consistent Malamute owner can teach his dog. While the Malamute may not leap to perform the first time you attempt to teach him something new, take heart. Once the lesson is mastered your Malamute will perform with enthusiasm and gusto that make all the hard work well worth while. Don't forget, you are dealing with one of the most strong-willed but also one of the most intelligent and wonderful breeds of dog known to man.

For advanced obedience work beyond the basics it is wise for the Malamute owner to consider local professional assistance. Professional trainers have long-standing experience in avoiding the pitfalls of obedience training and can help you to avoid them as well.

This training assistance can be obtained in many ways. Classes are particularly good for your Malamute's socialization. There are free-of-charge classes at many parks and recreation facilities, as well as very formal and sometimes very expensive individual lessons with private trainers.

Give your Malamute puppy plenty of safe chew toys, like Nylabones®, and he will be more likely to stay away from your socks!

There are also some obedience schools that will take your Malamute and train him for you. However, unless your schedule provides no time at all to train your own dog, having someone else train the dog for you would be last on our list of recommendations. The rapport that develops between the owner who has trained his or her Malamute to be a pleasant companion and good canine citizen is very special—well worth the time and patience it requires to achieve.

VERSATILITY

We call the Alaskan Malamute "the breed for all seasons and all reasons." The breed is ideal for athletic people, as Malamutes love to wear a pack and hike mountain trails with the family.

The breed is strong and has great endurance, making it an ideal candidate for sledding and skijorring. Skijorring is having your Malamute pull you along on your skis and it is difficult to determine who enjoys this more—the dog or the owner!

Any winter sport that employs your Malamute's ability to haul will suit the dog beyond measure. Those owners who do not live in the colder climates hitch their Malamutes to carts and traverse dirt roads and trails. Malamutes delight in showing off their talents in this area.

Alaskan Malamutes make wonderful show dogs, excelling in both the obedience and conformation rings. They love to perform.

The Alaskan Malamute's strength, endurance and love for the cold make them excellent candidates for training for winter sports like sledding and skijorring.

In Pullman, Washington, we have the "Bustad Buddies Program." The animals participating in this program are certified through the Delta Society, which is an international organization that oversees animal-assisting activities. Malamutes are providing assistance to people with physical handicaps of many kinds.

Malamutes are happy family pets and make wonderful therapy dogs for hospitals. The presence of Malamutes at rest homes inspires the elderly people there to share their memories of treasured pets they once owned. The rapport between these elderly folks and the Malamutes is delightful to witness.

Some rest homes and convalescent centers offer the services of the successful service inspired by Doctor Leo Bustad and the People-Pet Partnership. Locally, Sandy and Allen Shallbetter and their Malamute "Ladyhawke" make regular visits to the Pullman Memorial Hospital in Pullman, Washington, providing comfort and entertainment to young and old alike.

Dr. Leo Bustad, Allen Shallbetter and Ladyhawke are all active participants in the People-Pet Partnership, a program that provides regular visits to hospitalized patients.

SPORT of Purebred Dogs

by Judy Iby

Welcome to the exciting and sometimes frustrating sport of dogs. No doubt you are trying to learn more about dogs or you wouldn't be deep into this book. This section covers the basics that may entice you, further your knowledge and help you to understand the dog world. If you decide to give showing, obedience or any other dog activities a try, then I suggest you seek further help from the appropriate source.

Am. Can. Ch. Williwaw's Sunbear of Targhee, ROM, owned by Al and Mary Jane Holabach and Bill and Norma Dudley, is one of the breed's top winners with 13 Best in Show wins to his credit.

Dog showing has been a very popular sport for a long time and has been taken quite seriously by some. Others only enjoy it as a hobby.

The Kennel Club in England was formed in 1859, the American Kennel Club was established in 1884 and the Canadian Kennel Club was formed in 1888. The purpose of these clubs was to register purebred dogs and maintain their Stud Books. In the beginning, the concept of registering dogs was not readily accepted. More than 36 million dogs have been enrolled in the AKC Stud Book since its inception in 1888.

Presently the kennel clubs not only register dogs but adopt and enforce rules and regulations governing dog shows, obedience trials and field trials. Over the years they have fostered and encouraged interest in the health and welfare of the purebred dog. They routinely donate funds to veterinary research for study on genetic disorders.

Although best known as a sled dog, the Alaskan Malamute has not lost his hunting instincts.

Below are the addresses of the kennel clubs in the United States, Great Britain and Canada.

The American Kennel Club
51 Madison Avenue
New York, NY 10010
(Their registry is located at: 5580 Centerview Drive, STE 200, Raleigh, NC 27606-3390)

The Kennel Club
1 Clarges Street
Piccadilly, London, WIY 8AB, England

The Canadian Kennel Club
111 Eglinton Avenue
East Toronto, Ontario M6S 4V7
Canada

Today there are numerous activities that are enjoyable for both the dog and the handler. Some of the activities include conformation showing, obedience competition, tracking, agility, the Canine Good Citizen Certificate, and a wide range of instinct tests that vary from breed to breed. Where you start depends upon your goals which early on may not be readily apparent.

Puppy Kindergarten

Every puppy will benefit from this class. PKT is the foundation for all future dog activities from conformation to "couch potatoes." Pet owners should make an effort to attend even if they never expect to show their dog. The class is designed for puppies about three months of age with graduation at approximately five months of age. All the puppies will be in the same age group and, even though some may be a little unruly, there should not be any real problem. This class will teach the puppy some beginning obedience. As in all obedience classes the owner learns how to train his own dog. The PKT class gives the puppy the opportunity to interact with other puppies in the same age group and exposes him to strangers, which is very important. Some dogs grow up with behavior problems, one of them being fear of strangers. As you can see, there can be much to gain from this class.

There are some basic obedience exercises that every dog should learn. Some of these can be started with puppy kindergarten.

Sit

One way of teaching the sit is to have your dog on your left side with the leash in your right hand, close to the collar. Pull

Puppy kindergarten and obedience training will give your Malamute puppy an outlet to expend all his energy and keep him out of trouble.

up on the leash and at the same time reach around his hindlegs with your left hand and tuck them in. As you are doing this say, "Beau, sit." Always use the dog's name when you give an active command. Some owners like to use a treat holding it over the dog's head. The dog will need to sit to get the treat. Encourage the dog to hold the sit for a few seconds, which will eventually be the beginning of the Sit/Stay. Depending on how cooperative he is, you can rub him under the chin or stroke his back. It is a good time to establish eye contact.

With persistence and patience, your Alaskan Malamute will sit on command.

Down

Sit the dog on your left side and kneel down beside him with the leash in your right hand. Reach over him with your left hand and grasp his left foreleg. With your right hand, take his right foreleg and pull his legs forward while you say, "Beau, down." If he tries to get up, lean on his shoulder to encourage him to stay down. It will relax your dog if you stroke his back while he is down. Try to encourage him to stay down for a few seconds as preparation for the Down/Stay.

Heel

The definition of heeling is the dog walking under control at your left heel. Your puppy will learn controlled walking in the puppy kindergarten class, which will eventually lead to heeling. The command is "Beau, heel," and you start off briskly with your left foot. Your leash is in your right hand and your left hand is holding it about half way down. Your left hand should be able to control the leash and there should be a little slack in it. You want him to walk with you with your leg somewhere between his nose and his shoulder. You need to encourage him to stay with you, not forging (in front of you) or lagging behind you. It is best to keep him on a fairly short lead. Do not allow the lead to become tight. It is far better to give him a little jerk when necessary and remind him to heel. When you come to a halt, be prepared physically to make him sit. It takes practice to become coordinated. There are excellent books on training that you may wish to purchase. Your instructor should be able to recommend one for you.

Recall

This quite possibly is the most important exercise you will ever teach. It should be a pleasant experience. The puppy may learn to do random recalls while being attached to a long line such as a clothes line. *This Alaskan* Later the exercise will start with the dog *Malamute has* sitting and staying until called. The command *perfected the* is "Beau, come." Let your command be *"heel" and* happy. You want your dog to come willingly *awaits his next* and faithfully. The recall could save his life if *command.* he sneaks out the door. In practicing the recall, let him jump on you or touch you before you reach for him. If he is shy, then kneel down to his level. Reaching for the insecure dog could frighten him, and he may not be willing to come again in the future. Lots of praise and a treat would be in order whenever you do a recall. Under no circumstances should you ever correct your dog when he has come to you. Later in formal obedience your dog will be required to sit in front of you after recalling and then go to heel position.

CONFORMATION

Conformation showing is our oldest dog show sport. This type of showing is based on the dog's appearance—that is his structure, movement and attitude. When considering this type of showing, you need to be aware of your breed's standard and be able to evaluate your dog compared to that standard. The breeder of your puppy or other experienced breeders would be good sources for such an evaluation. Puppies can go through lots of changes over a period of time. I always say most puppies start out as promising hopefuls and then after maturing may be disappointing as show candidates. Even so this should not deter them from being excellent pets.

Usually conformation training classes are offered by the local kennel or obedience clubs. These are excellent places for training puppies. The puppy should be able to walk on a lead before entering such a class. Proper ring procedure and

technique for posing (stacking) the dog will be demonstrated as well as gaiting the dog. Usually certain patterns are used in the ring such as the triangle or the "L." Conformation class, like the PKT class, will give your youngster the opportunity to socialize with different breeds of dogs and humans too.

It takes some time to learn the routine of conformation showing. Usually one starts at the puppy matches which may be AKC Sanctioned or Fun Matches. These matches are generally for puppies from two or three months to a year old, and there may be classes for the adult over the age of 12 months. Similar to point shows, the classes are divided by sex and after completion of the classes in that breed or variety, the class winners compete for Best of Breed or Variety. The winner goes on to compete in the Group and the Group winners compete for Best in Match. No championship points are awarded for match wins.

A few matches can be great training for puppies even though there is no intention to go on showing. Matches enable the puppy to meet new people and be handled by a stranger—the judge. It is also a change of environment, which broadens the horizon for both dog and handler. Matches and other dog activities boost the confidence of the handler and especially the younger handlers.

Earning an AKC championship is built on a point system, which is different from Great Britain. To become an AKC Champion of Record the dog must earn 15 points. The number of points earned each time depends upon the number of dogs in competition. The number of points available at each show depends upon the breed, its sex and the location of the show. The United States is divided into ten AKC zones. Each zone has its own set of points. The purpose of the zones is to try to equalize the points available from breed to breed and area to area. The AKC adjusts the point scale annually.

Once your Malamute masters basic obedience, he can move on to more advanced and specialized activities, like sledding.

Hill Frost Quest For Fame, CDX, owned by Patty Padgett, clears the bar jump in an agility trial.

The number of points that can be won at a show are between one and five. Three-, four- and five-point wins are considered majors. Not only does the dog need 15 points won under three different judges, but those points must include two majors under two different judges. Canada also works on a point system but majors are not required.

Dogs always show before bitches. The classes available to those seeking points are: Puppy (which may be divided into 6 to 9 months and 9 to 12 months); 12 to 18 months; Novice; Bred-by-Exhibitor; American-bred; and Open. The class winners of the same sex of each breed or variety compete against each other for Winners Dog and Winners Bitch. A Reserve Winners Dog and Reserve Winners Bitch are also awarded but do not carry any points unless the Winners win is disallowed by AKC. The Winners Dog and Bitch compete with the specials (those dogs that have attained championship) for Best of Breed or Variety, Best of Winners and Best of Opposite Sex. It is possible to pick up an extra point or even a major if the points are higher for the defeated winner than those of

Best of Winners. The latter would get the higher total from the defeated winner.

At an all-breed show, each Best of Breed or Variety winner will go on to his respective Group and then the Group winners will compete against each other for Best in Show. There are seven Groups: Sporting, Hounds, Working, Terriers, Toys, Non-Sporting and Herding. Obviously there are no Groups at speciality shows (those shows that have only one breed or a show such as the American Spaniel Club's Flushing Spaniel Show, which is for all flushing spaniel breeds).

Earning a championship in England is somewhat different since they do not have a point system. Challenge Certificates are awarded if the judge feels the dog is deserving regardless of the number of dogs in competition. A dog must earn three Challenge Certificates under three different judges, with at least one of these Certificates being won after the age of 12 months. Competition is very strong and entries may be higher than they are in the U.S. The Kennel Club's Challenge Certificates are only available at Championship Shows.

In England, The Kennel Club regulations require that certain dogs, Border Collies and Gundog breeds, qualify in a working capacity (i.e., obedience or field trials) before becoming a full champion. If they do not qualify in the working aspect, then they are designated a Show Champion, which is equivalent to the AKC's Champion of Record. A Gundog may be granted the title of Field Trial Champion (FT Ch.) if it passes all the tests in the field but would also have to qualify in conformation before becoming a full Champion. A Border Collie that earns the title of Obedience Champion (Ob Ch.) must also qualify in the conformation ring before becoming a Champion.

The U.S. doesn't have a designation full Champion but does award for Dual and Triple Champions. The Dual Champion must be a Champion of Record, and either Champion Tracker, Herding Champion, Obedience Trial Champion or Field Champion. Any dog that has been awarded the titles of Champion of Record, and any two of the following: Champion Tracker, Herding Champion, Obedience Trial Champion or Field Champion, may be designated as a Triple Champion.

The shows in England seem to put more emphasis on breeder judges than those in the U.S. There is much competition within the breeds. Therefore the quality of the individual breeds should be very good. In the United States we tend to have more "all around judges" (those that judge multiple breeds) and use the breeder judges at the specialty shows. Breeder judges are more familiar with their own breed since they are actively breeding that breed or did so at one time. Americans emphasize Group and Best in Show wins and promote them accordingly.

It is my understanding that the shows in England can be very large and extend over several days, with the Groups being scheduled on different days. In our country we have cluster shows, where several different clubs will use the same show site over consecutive days.

Westminster Kennel Club is our most prestigious show although the entry is limited to 2500. In recent years, entry has been limited to Champions. This show is more formal than the majority of the shows with the judges wearing formal attire and the handlers fashionably dressed. In most instances the quality of the dogs is superb. After all, it is a show of Champions. It is a good show to study the AKC registered breeds and is by far the most exciting—especially since it is televised! WKC is one of the few shows in this country that is still benched. This means the dog must be in his benched area during

Alaskan Malamutes that compete in conformation must be perfectly groomed for presentation in the show ring.

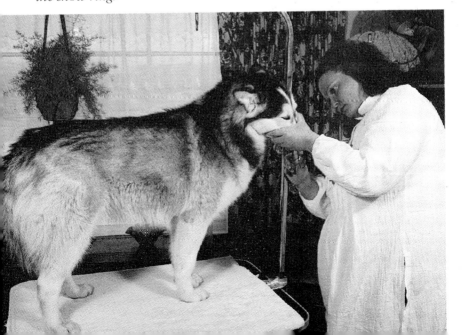

the show hours except when he is being groomed, in the ring, or being exercised.

Typically, the handlers are very particular about their appearances. They are careful not to wear something that will detract from their dog but will perhaps enhance it. American ring procedure is quite formal compared to that of other countries. I remember being reprimanded by a judge because I made a suggestion to a friend holding my second dog outside the ring. I certainly could have used more discretion so I would not call attention to myself. There is a certain etiquette expected between the judge and exhibitor and among the other exhibitors. Of course it is not always the case but the judge is supposed to be polite, not engaging in small talk or even acknowledging that he knows the handler. I understand that there is a more informal and relaxed atmosphere at the shows in other countries. For instance, the dress code is more casual. I can see where this might be more fun for the exhibitor and especially for the novice. This country is very handler-oriented in many of the breeds. It is true, in most instances, that the experienced professional handler can present the dog better and will have a feel for what a judge likes.

In England, Crufts is The Kennel Club's own show and is most assuredly the largest dog show in the world. They've been known to have an entry of nearly 20,000, and the show lasts four days. Entry is only gained by qualifying through winning in specified classes at another Championship Show. Westminster is strictly conformation, but Crufts exhibitors and spectators enjoy not only conformation but obedience, agility and a multitude of exhibitions as well. Obedience was admitted in 1957 and agility in 1983.

If you are handling your own dog, please give some consideration to your apparel. For sure the dress code at matches is more informal than the point shows. However, you should wear something a little more appropriate than beach attire or ragged jeans and bare feet. If you check out the handlers and see what is presently fashionable, you'll catch on. Men usually dress with a shirt and tie and a nice sports coat. Whether you are male or female, you will want to wear comfortable clothes and shoes. You need to be able to run with your dog and you certainly don't want to take a chance of falling and hurting yourself. Heaven forbid, if nothing else, you'll upset your dog. Women usually wear a dress or two-piece outfit, preferably with pockets to carry bait, comb, brush, etc. In this case men are the lucky ones with all their pockets. Ladies, think about where your dress will be if you need to kneel on the floor and also think about running. Does it allow freedom to do so?

Years ago, after toting around all the baby paraphernalia, I found toting the dog and necessities a breeze. You need to take along dog; crate; ex pen (if you use one); extra newspaper; water pail and water; all required grooming equipment, including hair dryer and extension cord; table; chair for you; bait for dog and lunch for you and friends; and, last but not least, clean up materials, such as plastic bags, paper towels, and perhaps a bath towel and some shampoo—just in case. Don't forget your entry confirmation and directions to the show.

An exercise pen is just one of the pieces of equipment you may need when traveling to a dog show. Snopaw's Nishga of Williwaw, CGC relaxes in her ex-pen.

If you are showing in obedience, then you will want to wear pants. Many of our top obedience handlers wear pants that are color-coordinated with their dogs. The philosophy is that imperfections in the black dog will be less obvious next to your black pants.

Whether you are showing in conformation, Junior Showmanship or obedience, you need to watch the clock and be sure you are not late. It is customary to pick up your conformation armband a few minutes before the start of the class. They will not wait for you and if you are on the show grounds and not in the ring, you will upset everyone. It's a

little more complicated picking up your obedience armband if you show later in the class. If you have not picked up your armband and they get to your number, you may not be allowed to show. It's best to pick up your armband early, but then you may show earlier than expected if other handlers don't pick up. Customarily all conflicts should be discussed with the judge prior to the start of the class.

Junior Showmanship

Your Malamute will enjoy trips to outdoor events and an exercise pen is a great way to keep him confined.

The Junior Showmanship Class is a wonderful way to build self confidence even if there are no aspirations of staying with the dog-show game later in life. Frequently, Junior Showmanship becomes the background of those who become successful exhibitors/handlers in the future. In some instances it is taken very seriously, and success is measured in terms of wins. The Junior Handler is judged solely on his ability and skill in presenting his dog. The dog's conformation is not to be considered by the judge. Even so the condition and grooming of the dog may be a reflection upon the handler.

Usually the matches and point shows include different classes. The Junior Handler's dog may be entered in a breed or obedience class and even shown by another person in that class. Junior Showmanship classes are usually divided by age and perhaps sex. The age is determined by the handler's age on the day of the show. The classes are: Novice Junior, Novice Senior, Open Junior, Open Senior.

Alaskan Malamutes are a bundle of energy. It is best to get them involved in activities— like shoveling the walk!

CANINE GOOD CITIZEN

The AKC sponsors a program to encourage dog owners to train their dogs. Local clubs perform the pass/fail tests, and dogs who pass are awarded a Canine Good Citizen Certificate. Proof of vaccination is required at the time of

participation. The test includes:
1. Accepting a friendly stranger.
2. Sitting politely for petting.
3. Appearance and grooming.
4. Walking on a loose leash.
5. Walking through a crowd.
6. Sit and down on command/staying in place.
7. Come when called.
8. Reaction to another dog.
9. Reactions to distractions.
10. Supervised separation.

If more effort was made by pet owners to accomplish these exercises, fewer dogs would be cast off to the humane shelter.

OBEDIENCE

Obedience is necessary, without a doubt, but it can also become a wonderful hobby or even an obsession. In my opinion, obedience classes and competition can provide wonderful companionship, not only with your dog but with your classmates or fellow competitors. It is always gratifying to discuss your dog's problems with others who have had similar experiences. The AKC acknowledged Obedience around 1936, and it has changed tremendously even though many of the exercises are basically the same. Today, obedience competition is just that—very competitive. Even so, it is possible for every obedience exhibitor to come home a winner (by earning qualifying scores) even though he/she may not earn a placement in the class.

Puppies learn a lot from other puppies, especially how to get along with each other! This is why puppy kindergarten is so beneficial.

Most of the obedience titles are awarded after earning three qualifying scores (legs) in the appropriate class under three different judges. These classes offer a perfect score of 200, which is extremely rare. Each of the class exercises has its own point value. A leg is earned after receiving a score of at least 170 and at least 50 percent of the points available in each exercise. The titles are:

The authors' "Ivaloo" looks back to see who might be ready to join her in a winter romp.

Companion Dog–CD
Companion Dog Excellent–CDX
Utility Dog–UD

After achieving the UD title, you may feel inclined to go after the UDX and/or OTCh. The UDX (Utility Dog Excellent) title went into effect in January 1994. It is not easily attained. The title requires qualifying simultaneously ten times in Open B and Utility B but not necessarily at consecutive shows.

The OTCh (Obedience Trial Champion) is awarded after the dog has earned his UD and then goes on to earn 100 championship points, a first place in Utility, a first place in Open and another first place in either class. The placements must be won under three different judges at all-breed obedience trials. The points are determined by the number of dogs competing in the Open B and Utility B classes. The OTCh title precedes the dog's name.

Obedience matches (AKC Sanctioned, Fun, and Show and Go) are usually available. Usually they are sponsored by the local obedience clubs. When preparing an obedience dog for a title, you will find matches very helpful. Fun Matches and Show and Go Matches are more lenient in allowing you to make corrections in the ring. I frequently train (correct) in the ring and inform the judge that I would like to do so and to please mark me "exhibition." This means that I will not be eligible for any prize. This type of training is usually very necessary for the Open and Utility Classes. AKC Sanctioned Obedience Matches do not allow corrections in the ring since they must abide by the AKC Obedience Regulations. If you are interested in showing in obedience, then you should contact the AKC for a copy of the Obedience Regulations.

TRACKING

Tracking is officially classified obedience, but I feel it should have its own category. There are three tracking titles available: Tracking Dog (TD), Tracking Dog Excellent (TDX), Variable Surface Tracking (VST). If all three tracking titles are obtained, then the dog officially becomes a CT (Champion Tracker). The CT will go in front of the dog's name.

A TD may be earned anytime and does not have to follow the other obedience titles. There are many exhibitors that prefer tracking to obedience, and there are others like myself that do both. In my experience with small dogs, I prefer to earn the CD and CDX before attempting tracking. My reasoning is that small dogs are closer to the mat in the obedience rings and therefore it's too easy to put the nose down and sniff. Tracking encourages sniffing. Of course this depends on the dog. I've had some dogs that tracked around the ring and others (TDXs) who wouldn't think of sniffing in the ring.

Agility is an action-packed sport that thrills both dogs and spectators. Hyak tries her hand at the teeter-totter.

The versatility and athleticism of the Alaskan Malamute make him a natural contender in the sport of agility. Hyak flies through the tire jump.

AGILITY

Agility was first introduced by John Varley in England at the Crufts Dog Show, February 1978, but Peter Meanwell, competitor and judge, actually developed the idea. It was officially recognized in the early '80s. Agility is extremely popular in England and Canada and growing in popularity in the U.S. The AKC acknowledged agility in August 1994. Dogs must be at least 12 months of age to be entered. It is a fascinating sport that the dog, handler and spectators enjoy to the utmost. Agility is a spectator sport! The dog performs off lead. The handler either runs with his dog or positions himself on the course and directs his dog with verbal and hand signals over a timed course over or through a variety of obstacles including a time out or pause. One of the main drawbacks to agility is finding a place to train. The obstacles take up a lot of space and it is very time consuming to put up and take down courses.

The titles earned at AKC agility trials are Novice Agility Dog (NAD), Open Agility Dog (OAD), Agility Dog Excellent (ADX), and Master Agility Excellent (MAX). In order to acquire an agility title, a dog must earn a qualifying score in its respective class on three separate occasions under two different *Although Tundra's long, soft coat is not correct for a show or breeding Malamute, that does not stop him from being the beloved companion of Warren and Dorothy Peterson.* judges. The MAX will be awarded after earning ten qualifying scores in the Agility Excellent Class.

PERFORMANCE TESTS

During the last decade the American Kennel Club has promoted performance tests–those events that test the different breeds' natural abilities. This type of event encourages a handler to devote even more time to his dog and retain the natural instincts of his breed heritage. It is an important part of the wonderful world of dogs.

GENERAL INFORMATION

Obedience, tracking and agility allow the purebred dog with an Indefinite Listing Privilege (ILP) number or a limited registration to be exhibited and earn titles. Application must be made to the AKC for an ILP number.

The American Kennel Club publishes a monthly *Events* magazine that is part of the *Gazette*, their official journal for the sport of purebred dogs. The *Events* section lists upcoming shows and the secretary or superintendent for them. The majority of the conformation shows in the U.S. are overseen by licensed superintendents. Generally the entry closing date is approximately two-and-a-half weeks before the actual show. Point shows are fairly expensive, while the match shows cost about one third of the point show entry fee. Match shows usually take entries the day of the show but some are pre-entry. The best way to find match show information is through your local kennel club. Upon asking, the AKC can

Performance tests measure a breed's natural abilities and help to retain its instincts and heritage. Allen Shallbetter and his team doing what they do best.

provide you with a list of superintendents, and you can write and ask to be put on their mailing lists.

Obedience trial and tracking test information is available through the AKC. Frequently these events are not superintended, but put on by the host club. Therefore you would make the entry with the event's secretary.

As you have read, there are numerous activities you can share with your dog. Regardless what you do, it does take teamwork. Your dog can only benefit from your attention and training. I hope this chapter has enlightened you and hope, if nothing else, you will attend a show here and there. Perhaps you will start with a puppy kindergarten class, and who knows where it may lead!

BEHAVIOR and Canine Communication

by Judy Iby

S tudies of the human/animal bond point out the importance of the unique relationships that exist between people and their pets. Those of us who share our lives with pets understand the special part they play through companionship, service and protection. For many, the pet/owner bond goes beyond simple companionship; pets are often considered members of the family. A leading pet food manufacturer recently conducted a nationwide survey of pet owners to gauge just how important pets were in their lives. Here's what they found:

- 76 percent allow their pets to sleep on their beds
- 78 percent think of their pets as their children
- 84 percent display photos of their pets, mostly in their homes.
- 100 percent talk to their pets
- 97 percent think that their pets understand what they're saying

The majority of Alaskan Malamutes live in family environments and have to conform to the rules of the household —which may mean no sitting on the furniture!

"Dreams of the Klondike." Carolyn Hays's "Parka" is lost in contemplation of those good-old-bad-old days in the tundra.

Are you surprised?

Senior citizens show more concern for their own eating habits when they have the responsibility of feeding a dog. Seeing that their dog is routinely exercised encourages the owner to think of schedules that otherwise may seem unimportant to the senior citizen. The older owner may be arthritic and feeling poorly but with responsibility for his dog he has a reason to get up and get moving. It is a big plus if his dog is an attention seeker who will demand such from his owner.

Over the last couple of decades, it has been shown that pets relieve the stress of those who lead busy lives. Owning a pet has been known to lessen the occurrence of heart attack and stroke.

Many single folks thrive on the companionship of a dog. Lifestyles are very different from a long time ago, and today more individuals seek the single life. However, they receive fulfillment from owning a dog.

Most likely the majority of our dogs live in family

environments. The companionship they provide is well worth the effort involved. In my opinion, every child should have the opportunity to have a family dog. Dogs teach responsibility through understanding their care, feelings and even respecting their life cycles. Frequently those children who have not been exposed to dogs grow up afraid of dogs, which isn't good. Dogs sense timidity and some will take advantage of the situation.

Today more dogs are serving as service dogs. Since the origination of the Seeing Eye dogs years ago, we now have trained hearing dogs. Also dogs are trained to provide service for the handicapped and are able to perform many different tasks for their owners. Search and Rescue dogs, with their handlers, are sent throughout the world to assist in recovery of disaster victims. They are life savers.

Well-socialized Malamutes should be able to play with each other without showing fear or aggression.

Therapy dogs are very popular with nursing homes, and some hospitals even allow them to visit. The inhabitants truly look forward to their visits. I have taken a couple of my dogs visiting and left in tears when I saw the response of the patients. They wanted and were allowed to have my dogs in their beds to hold and love.

Nationally there is a Pet Awareness Week to educate students and others about the value and basic care of our pets. Many countries take an even greater interest in their pets than Americans do. In those countries the pets are allowed to accompany their owners into restaurants and shops, etc. In the U.S. this freedom is only available to our service dogs. Even so we think very highly of the human/animal bond.

CANINE BEHAVIOR

Canine behavior problems are the number-one reason for

With patience, love and commitment, the bond between owner and Malamute can be a strong one.

pet owners to dispose of their dogs, either through new homes, humane shelters or euthanasia. Unfortunately there are too many owners who are unwilling to devote the necessary time to properly train their dogs. On the other hand, there are those who not only are concerned about inherited health problems but are also aware of the dog's mental stability.

You may realize that a breed and his group relatives (i.e., sporting, hounds, etc.) show tendencies to behavioral characteristics. An experienced breeder can acquaint you with his breed's personality. Unfortunately many breeds are labeled with poor temperaments when actually the breed as a whole is not affected but only a small percentage of individuals within the breed.

If the breed in question is very popular, then of course there may be a higher number of unstable dogs. Do not label a breed

good or bad. I know of absolutely awful-tempered dogs within one of our most popular, lovable breeds.

Inheritance and environment contribute to the dog's behavior. Some naïve people suggest inbreeding as the cause of bad temperaments. Inbreeding only results in poor behavior if the ancestors carry the trait. If there are excellent temperaments behind the dogs, then inbreeding will promote good temperaments in the offspring. Did you ever consider that inbreeding is what sets the characteristics of a breed? A purebred dog is the end result of inbreeding. This does not spare the mixed-breed dog from the same problems. Mixed-breed dogs frequently are the offspring of purebred dogs.

When planning a breeding, I like to observe the potential stud and his offspring in the show ring. If I see unruly behavior, I try to look into it further. I want to know if it is genetic or environmental, due to the lack of training and socialization. A good breeder will avoid breeding mentally unsound dogs.

Although all members of a certain breed share similarities, every Malamute is an individual and should be treated as such.

Not too many decades ago most of our dogs led a different lifestyle than what is prevalent today. Usually mom stayed home so the dog had human companionship and someone to discipline it if needed. Not much was expected from the dog. Today's mom works and everyone's life is at a much faster pace.

The dog may have to adjust to being a "weekend" dog. The family is gone all day during the week, and the dog is left to his own devices for entertainment. Some dogs sleep all day waiting for their family to come home and others become wigwam wreckers if given the opportunity. Crates do ensure the safety of the dog and the house. However, he could become a physically and emotionally cripple if he doesn't get enough exercise and attention. We still appreciate and want the companionship of our dogs although we expect more from them.

Different breeds have different inherent characteristics. This Malamute howls at the moon.

In many cases we tend to forget dogs are just that—*dogs* not human beings.

I own several dogs who are left crated during the day but I do try to make time for them in the evenings and on the weekends. Also we try to do something together before I leave for work. Maybe it helps them to have the companionship of other dogs. They accept their crates as their personal "houses" and seem to be content with their routine and thrive on trying their best to please me.

Socializing and Training

Many prospective puppy buyers lack experience regarding the proper socialization and training needed to develop the type of pet we all desire. In the first 18 months, training does take some work. Trust me, it is easier to start proper training before there is a problem that needs to be corrected.

The initial work begins with the breeder. The breeder should start socializing the puppy at five to six weeks of age and cannot let up. Human socializing is critical up through 12

Although a large sized dog, a well-trained and properly socialized Alaskan Malamute can make a great housepet.

weeks of age and likewise important during the following months. The litter should be left together during the first few weeks but it is necessary to separate them by ten weeks of age. Leaving them together after that time will increase competition for litter dominance. If puppies are not socialized with people by 12 weeks of age, they may be timid in later life.

The eight- to ten-week age period is a fearful time for puppies. They need to be handled very gently around children and adults. There should be no harsh discipline during this time. Starting at 14 weeks of age, the puppy begins the juvenile period, which ends when he reaches sexual maturity around six to 14 months of age. During the juvenile period he needs to be introduced to strangers (adults, children and other dogs) on the home property. At sexual maturity he will begin to bark at strangers and become more protective. Males start to lift their legs to urinate but if you desire you can inhibit this behavior by walking your boy on leash away from trees, shrubs, fences, etc.

Coax your Malamute puppy out of his fearful stage by introducing him to as many gentle people and animals as possible and by offering him a Nylabone® to chew on.

Perhaps you are thinking about an older puppy. You need to inquire about the puppy's social experience. If he has lived in a kennel, he may have a hard time adjusting to people and environmental stimuli. Assuming he has had a good social upbringing, there are advantages to an older puppy.

Training includes puppy kindergarten and a minimum of one to two basic training classes. During these classes you will learn how to train your youngster. This is especially important if you own a large breed of dog. It is somewhat harder, if not nearly impossible, for some owners to be the Alpha figure when their dog towers over them. You will be taught how to properly restrain your dog. This concept is important. Again it puts you in the Alpha position. All dogs need to be restrained many times during their lives. Believe it or not, some of our worst offenders are the eight-week-old puppies that are

One of the most important aspects of a dog's upbringing is socialization with all kinds of animals. Cats and Malamutes will get along fine if properly introduced.

brought to our clinic. They need to be gently restrained for a nail trim but the way they carry on you would think we were killing them. In comparison, their vaccination is a "piece of cake." When we ask dogs to do something that is not agreeable to them, then their worst comes out. Life will be easier for your dog if you expose him at a young age to the necessities of life–proper behavior and restraint.

Understanding the Dog's Language

Most authorities agree that the dog is a descendent of the wolf. The dog and wolf have similar traits. For instance both are pack oriented and prefer not to be isolated for long periods of time. Another characteristic is that the dog, like the wolf, looks to the leader—Alpha—for direction. Both the wolf and the dog communicate through body language, not only within their pack but with outsiders.

Every pack has an Alpha figure. The dog looks to you, or should look to you, to be that leader. If your dog doesn't receive the proper training and guidance, he very well may replace you as Alpha. This would be a serious problem and is certainly a disservice to your dog.

Eye contact is one way the Alpha wolf keeps order within his pack. You are Alpha, so you must establish eye contact with your puppy. Obviously your puppy will have to look at you. Practice eye contact even if you need to hold his head for five to ten seconds at a time. You can give him a treat as a reward. Make sure

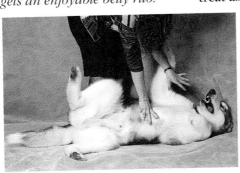

An Alaskan Malamute on his back, belly exposed, submits to his owner's dominant role —and gets an enjoyable belly rub!

your eye contact is gentle and not threatening. Later, if he has been naughty, it is permissible to give him a long, penetrating look. There are some older dogs that never learned eye contact as puppies and cannot accept eye contact. You should avoid eye contact with these dogs since they feel threatened and may retaliate as such.

BODY LANGUAGE

The play bow, when the forequarters are down and the hindquarters are elevated, is an invitation to play. Puppies play fight, which helps them learn the acceptable limits of biting. This is necessary for later in their lives. Nevertheless, an owner may be falsely reassured by the playful nature of his dog's aggression. Playful aggression toward another dog or human may be an indication of serious aggression in the future. Owners should never play fight or play tug-of-war with any dog that is inclined to be dominant.

Signs of submission are:

1. Avoids eye contact.

2. Active submission—the dog crouches down, ears back and the tail is lowered.

3. Passive submission—the dog rolls on his side with his hindlegs in the air and frequently urinates.

Signs of dominance are:

1. Makes eye contact.

2. Stands with ears up, tail up and the hair raised on his neck.

3. Shows dominance over another dog by standing at right angles over it.

Dominant dogs tend to behave in characteristic ways such as:

1. The dog may be unwilling to move from his place (i.e., reluctant to give up the sofa if the owner wants to sit there).

2. He may not part with toys or objects in his mouth and may show possessiveness with his food bowl.

3. He may not respond quickly to commands.

4. He may be disagreeable for grooming and dislikes to be petted.

Dogs are popular because of their sociable nature. Those that have contact with humans during the first 12 weeks of life regard them as a member of their own species—their pack. All dogs have the potential for both dominant and submissive behavior. Only through experience and training do they learn to whom it is appropriate to show which behavior. Not all dogs are concerned with dominance but owners need to be aware of that potential. It is wise for the owner to establish his dominance early on.

A human can express dominance or submission toward a dog in the following ways:

1. Meeting the dog's gaze signals dominance. Averting the gaze signals submission. If the dog growls or threatens, averting the gaze is the first avoiding action to take—it may prevent attack. It is important to establish eye contact in the puppy. The older dog that has not been exposed to eye contact may see it as a threat and will not be willing to submit.

2. Being taller than the dog signals dominance; being

lower signals submission. This is why, when attempting to make friends with a strange dog or catch the runaway, one should kneel down to his level. Some owners see their dogs become dominant when allowed on the furniture or on the bed. Then he is at the owner's level.

3. An owner can gain dominance by ignoring all the dog's social initiatives. The owner pays attention to the dog only when he obeys a command.

No dog should be allowed to achieve dominant status over any adult or child. Ways of preventing are as follows:

1. Handle the puppy gently, especially during the three- to four-month period.

2. Let the children and adults handfeed him and teach him to take food without lunging or grabbing.

3. Do not allow him to chase children or joggers.

4. Do not allow him to jump on people or mount their legs. Even females may be inclined to mount. It is not only a male habit.

With Nylafloss®, puppies can play tug-of-war games and clean their teeth and gums at the same time!

5. Do not allow him to growl for any reason.

6. Don't participate in wrestling or tug-of-war games.

7. Don't physically punish puppies for aggressive behavior.

Restrain him from repeating the infraction and teach an alternative behavior. Dogs should earn everything they receive from their owners. This would include sitting to receive petting or treats, sitting before going out the door and sitting to receive the collar and leash. These types of exercises reinforce the owner's dominance.

Young children should never be left alone with a dog. It is important that children learn some basic obedience commands so they have some control over the dog. They will gain the respect of their dog.

Fear

One of the most common problems dogs experience is being fearful. Some dogs are more afraid than others. On the lesser side, which is sometimes humorous to watch, my dog can be afraid of a strange object. He acts silly when something is out of place in the house. I call his problem perceptive intelligence. He realizes the abnormal within his known environment. He does not react the same way in strange environments since he does not know what is normal.

On the more serious side is a fear of people. This can result in backing off, seeking his own space and saying "leave me alone" or it can result in an aggressive behavior that may lead to challenging the person. Respect that the dog wants to be left alone and give him time to come forward. If you approach the cornered dog, he may resort to snapping. If you leave him alone, he may decide to come forward, which should be rewarded with a treat. Years ago we had a dog that behaved in this manner. We coaxed people to stop by the house and make friends with our fearful dog. She learned to take the treats and after weeks of work she overcame her suspicions and made friends more readily.

Some dogs may initially be too fearful to take treats. In these cases it is helpful to make sure the dog hasn't eaten for about 24 hours. Being a little hungry encourages him to accept the treats, especially if they are of the "gourmet" variety. I have a dog that worries about strangers since people seldom stop by my house. Over the years she has learned a cue and jumps up quickly to visit anyone sitting on the sofa.

"The gang's all here!" Bill and Debbie Griffith's Malamute sextet pose for the camera after a weekend frolic in the snow.

She learned by herself that all guests on the sofa were to be trusted friends. I think she felt more comfortable with them being at her level, rather than towering over her.

Dogs can be afraid of numerous things, including loud noises and thunderstorms. Invariably the owner rewards (by comforting) the dog when it shows signs of fearfulness. I had a terrible problem with my favorite dog in the Utility obedience class. Not only was he intimidated in the class but he was afraid of noise and afraid of displeasing me. Frequently he would knock down the bar jump, which clattered dreadfully. I gave him credit because he continued to try to clear it, although he was terribly scared. I finally learned to "reward" him every time he knocked down the jump. I would jump up and down, clap my hands and tell him how great he was. My psychology worked, he relaxed and eventually cleared the jump with ease. When your dog is frightened, direct his attention to something else and act happy. Don't dwell on his fright.

Give your Malamute lots of praise and treats like a Hercules® bone when he obeys you. This positive reinforcement will ensure your dog will be eager to please.

AGGRESSION

Some different types of aggression are: predatory, defensive, dominance, possessive, protective, fear induced, noise provoked, "rage" syndrome (unprovoked aggression), maternal and aggression directed toward other dogs. Aggression is the most common behavioral problem encountered. Protective breeds are expected to be more aggressive than others but with the proper upbringing they can make very dependable companions. You need to be able to read your dog.

Many factors contribute to aggression including genetics and environment. An improper environment, which may include the living conditions, lack of social life, excessive punishment, being attacked or frightened by an aggressive dog, etc., can all influence a dog's behavior. Even spoiling him and giving too much praise may be detrimental. Isolation and the lack of human contact or exposure to frequent teasing by children or adults also can ruin a good dog.

Lack of direction, fear, or confusion lead to aggression in those dogs that are so inclined. Any obedience exercise, even the sit and down, can direct the dog and overcome fear and/or confusion. Every dog should learn these commands as a youngster, and there should be periodic reinforcement.

When a dog is showing signs of aggression, you should speak calmly (no screaming or hysterics) and firmly give a command that he understands, such as the sit. As soon as your dog obeys, you have assumed your dominant position. Aggression presents a problem because there may be danger to others. Sometimes it is an emotional issue. Owners may consciously or unconsciously encourage their dog's aggression. Other owners show responsibility by accepting the problem and taking measures to keep it under control. The owner is responsible for his dog's actions, and it is not wise to take a chance on someone being bitten, especially a child. Euthanasia is the solution for some owners and in severe cases this may be the best choice. However, few dogs are that dangerous and very few are that much of a threat to their owners. If caution is exercised and professional help is gained early on, then I surmise most cases can be controlled.

Some authorities recommend feeding a lower protein (less than 20 percent) diet. They believe this can aid in reducing aggression. If the dog loses weight, then vegetable oil can be added. Veterinarians and behaviorists are having some success

If you allow your Alaskan Malamute to develop a bad habit, like lying on the bed, it will be hard to break him of it later on.

with pharmacology. In many cases treatment is possible and can improve the situation.

If you have done everything according to "the book" regarding training and socializing and are still having a behavior problem, don't procrastinate. It is important that the problem gets attention before it is out of hand. It is estimated that 20 percent of a veterinarian's time may be devoted to dealing with problems before they become so intolerable that the dog is separated from its home and owner. If your veterinarian isn't able to help, he should refer you to a behaviorist.

A well-mannered Alaskan Malamute is a pleasure to own and will be welcomed wherever he goes. This is Winter Legacy, owned by the author.

Malamute youngsters love to chew, so keep them from being destructive by offering them Nylabones®.

Problems

Barking

Although some Malmutes rarely, if ever, bark, this is a habit that shouldn't be encouraged. Over the years I've had new puppy owners call to say that their dog hasn't learned to bark. I assure them they are indeed fortunate but not to worry. Some owners desire their dog to bark so as to be a watchdog. In my experience, most dogs will bark when a stranger comes to the door.

The new puppy frequently barks or whines in the crate in his strange environment and the owner reinforces the puppy's bad behavior by going to him during the night. This is a no-no. I tell my new owners to smack the top of the crate and say "quiet" in a loud, firm voice. The puppies don't like to hear the loud noise of the crate being banged. If the barking is sleep-interrupting, then the owner should take crate and pup to the bedroom for a few days until the puppy becomes adjusted to his new environment. Otherwise ignore the barking during the night.

Barking can be an inherited problem or a bad habit learned through the environment. It takes dedication to stop the barking. Attention should be paid to the cause of the barking. Does the dog seek attention, does he need to go out, is it feeding time, is it occurring when he is left alone, is it a protective bark, etc.? Presently I have a ten-week-old puppy that is a real loud mouth, which I am sure is an inherited tendency. Both her mother and especially her grandmother are overzealous barkers but fortunately have mellowed with the years. My young puppy is corrected with a firm "no" and gentle shaking and she is responding. When barking presents a problem for you, try to stop it as soon as it begins.

There are electronic collars available that are supposed to curb barking. Personally I have not had experience with them. There are some disadvantages to the collar. If the dog is barking out of excitement, punishment is not the appropriate treatment. Presumably there is the chance the collar could be activated by other stimuli and thereby punish the dog when it is not barking. Should you decide to use one, then you should seek help from a person with experience with that type of collar. In my opinion I feel the root of the problem needs to be investigated and corrected.

In extreme circumstances (usually when there is a problem with the neighbors), some people have resorted to having their dogs debarked. I caution you that the dog continues to bark but usually only a squeaking sound is heard. Frequently the vocal cords grow back. Probably the biggest concern is that the dog can be left with scar tissue which can narrow the opening to the trachea.

Jumping Up

Personally, I am not thrilled when other dogs jump on me but I have hurt feelings if they don't! I do encourage my own dogs to jump on me, on command. Some do and some don't. In my opinion, a dog that jumps up is a happy dog. Nevertheless few guests appreciate dogs jumping on them. Clothes get footprinted and/or snagged.

Alaskan Malamutes are an independent breed with a tendency to wander. Make sure your dogs are in a secure fenced-in area when outside.

I am a believer in allowing the puppy to jump up during his first few weeks. In my opinion if you correct him too soon and at the wrong age you may intimidate him. Consequently he could be timid around humans later in his life. However, there will come a time, probably around four months of age, that he needs to know when it is okay to jump and when he is to show off good manners by sitting instead.

Some authorities never allow jumping. If you are irritated by your dog jumping up on you, then you should discourage it from the beginning. A larger breed of dog can cause harm to a senior citizen. Some are quite fragile. It may not take much to cause a topple that could break a hip.

How do you correct the problem? All family members need to participate in teaching the puppy to sit as soon as he starts to jump up. The sit must be practiced every time he starts to jump up. Don't forget to praise him for his good behavior. If an older dog has acquired the habit, grasp his paws and squeeze tightly. Give a firm "No." He'll soon catch on. Remember the entire family must take part. Each time you allow him to jump up you go back a step in training.

Biting

All puppies bite and try to chew on your fingers, toes, arms, etc. This is the time to teach them to be gentle and not bite hard. Put your fingers in your puppy's mouth and if he bites too hard then say "easy" and let him know he's hurting you. I squeal and act like I have been seriously hurt. If the puppy plays too rough and doesn't respond to your corrections, then he needs "Time Out" in his crate. You should be particularly careful with young children and puppies who still have their deciduous (baby) teeth. Those teeth are like needles and can leave little scars on youngsters.

Biting in the more mature dog is something that should be prevented at all costs. Should it occur I would quickly let him know in no uncertain terms that biting will not be tolerated. When biting is directed toward another dog (dog fight), don't get in the middle of it. On more than one occasion I have had to separate a couple of my dogs and usually was in the middle of that one last lunge by the offender. Some authorities recommend breaking up a fight by elevating the hind legs. This would only be possible if there was a person for each dog. Obviously it would be hard to fight with the hind legs off the ground. A dog bite is serious and should be given attention.

Biting is very common in young puppies but unacceptable in adult Malamutes. Curb your pup's tendency to chew early on.

Wash the bite with soap and water and contact your doctor. It is important to know the status of the offender's rabies vaccination.

Though little "Destiny" is only 12 weeks old, she has that digging instinct that all Malamutes are born with.

I have several dogs that are sensitive to having mats combed out of their coats and eventually they have had enough. They give fair warning by turning and acting like they would like to nip my offending fingers. However, one verbal warning from me says, "I'm sorry, don't you dare think about biting me and please let me carefully comb just a little bit more." I have owned a minimum of 30 dogs and raised many more puppies and have yet to have one of my dogs bite me except during that last lunge in the two or three dog fights I felt compelled to break up. My dogs wouldn't dare bite me. They know who is boss.

This is not always the case for other owners. I do not wish to frighten you but when biting occurs you should seek professional help at once. On the other hand you must not let your dog intimidate you and be so afraid of a bite that you can't discipline him. Professional help through your veterinarian, dog trainer and/or behaviorist can give you guidance.

Digging

Bored dogs release their frustrations through mischievous behavior such as digging. For the life of me I do not understand why people own dogs only to keep them outside. Dogs shouldn't be left unattended outside, even if they are in a fenced-in yard. Usually the dog is sent to "jail" (the backyard) because the owner can't tolerate him in the house. The culprit feels socially deprived and needs to be included in the owner's life. The owner has neglected the dog's training. The dog has not developed into the companion we desire. If you are one of these owners, then perhaps it is possible for you to change. Give him another chance. Some owners object to their dog's unkempt coat and doggy odor. See that he is groomed on a regular schedule and look into some training classes.

HEALTH CARE

by Judy Iby

Veterinary medicine has become far more sophisticated than what was available to our ancestors. This can be attributed to the increase in household pets and consequently the demand for better care for them. Also human medicine has become far more complex. Today diagnostic testing in veterinary medicine parallels human diagnostics. Because of better technology we can expect our pets to live healthier lives thereby increasing their life spans.

A healthy Alaskan Malamute will be able to participate in his favorite activities–mainly playing in the snow.

Puppies receive maternal antibodies that protect them from diseases for the first few weeks of life. Vaccinations are needed at an early age because the antibodies are only temporary.

THE FIRST CHECK UP

You will want to take your new puppy/dog in for its first check up within 24 to 72 hours after acquiring it. Many breeders strongly recommend this check up and so do the humane shelters. A puppy/dog

can appear healthy but it may have a serious problem that is not apparent to the layman. Most pets have some type of a minor flaw that may never cause a real problem.

Unfortunately if he/she should have a serious problem, you will want to consider the consequences of keeping the pet and the attachments that will be formed, which may be broken prematurely. Keep in mind there are many healthy dogs looking for good homes.

This first check up is a good time to establish yourself with the veterinarian and learn the office policy regarding their hours and how they handle emergencies. Usually the breeder or another conscientious pet owner is a good reference for locating a capable veterinarian. You should be aware that not all veterinarians give the same quality of service. Please do not make your selection on the least expensive clinic, as they may be short changing your pet. There is the possibility that eventually it will cost you more due to improper diagnosis, treatment, etc. If you are selecting a new veterinarian, feel free to ask for a tour of the clinic. You should inquire about making an appointment for a tour since all clinics are working clinics, and therefore may not be available all day for sightseers. You may worry less if you see where your pet will be spending the day if he ever needs to be hospitalized.

These six-week-old Malamute pups are ready for their first set of vaccinations.

THE PHYSICAL EXAM

Your veterinarian will check your pet's overall condition, which includes listening to the heart; checking the respiration; feeling the abdomen, muscles and joints; checking the mouth, which includes the gum color and signs of gum disease along with plaque buildup; checking the ears for signs of an infection or ear mites; examining the eyes; and, last but not least, checking the condition of the skin and coat.

Your Alaskan Malamute puppy will look to you, his owner, to provide him with the health care he requires.

133

He should ask you questions regarding your pet's eating and elimination habits and invite you to relay your questions. It is a good idea to prepare a list so as not to forget anything. He should discuss the proper diet and the quantity to be fed. If this should differ from your breeder's recommendation, then you should convey to him the breeder's choice and see if he approves. If he recommends changing the diet, then this should be done over a few days so as not to cause a gastrointestinal upset. It is customary to take in a fresh stool sample (just a small amount) for a test for intestinal parasites. It must be fresh, preferably within 12 hours, since the eggs hatch quickly and after hatching will not be observed under the microscope. If your pet isn't obliging then, usually the technician can take one in the clinic.

When you take your Malamute home, the breeder should give you a diet sheet explaining the puppy's feeding schedule and the proper diet.

IMMUNIZATIONS
It is important that you take your puppy/dog's vaccination record with you on your first visit. In case of a puppy, presumably the breeder has seen to the vaccinations up to the time you acquired custody. Veterinarians differ in their vaccination protocol. It is not unusual for your puppy to have received vaccinations for distemper, hepatitis, leptospirosis, parvovirus and parainfluenza every two to three weeks from the age of five or six weeks. Usually this is a combined injection and is typically called the DHLPP. The DHLPP is given through at least 12 to 14 weeks of age, and it is customary to continue with another parvovirus vaccine at 16 to 18 weeks. You may wonder why so many immunizations are necessary. No one knows for sure when the puppy's maternal antibodies are gone, although it is customarily accepted that distemper antibodies are gone by 12 weeks.

Immunizations will protect your vulnerable Malamute puppy from many life-threatening diseases.

Usually parvovirus antibodies are gone by 16 to 18 weeks of age. However, it is possible for the maternal antibodies to be gone at a much earlier age or even a later age. Therefore immunizations are started at an early age. The vaccine will not give immunity as long as there are maternal antibodies.

The rabies vaccination is given at three or six months of age depending on your local laws. A vaccine for bordetella (kennel cough) is available and can be given anytime from the age of five weeks. The coronavirus is not commonly given unless there is a problem locally. The Lyme vaccine is necessary in endemic areas. Lyme disease has been reported in 47 states.

Distemper

This is virtually an incurable disease. If the dog recovers, he is subject to severe nervous disorders. The virus attacks every tissue in the body and resembles a bad cold with a fever. It can cause a runny nose and eyes and cause gastrointestinal disorders, including a poor appetite, vomiting and diarrhea. The virus is carried by raccoons, foxes, wolves, mink and other dogs. Unvaccinated youngsters and senior citizens are very susceptible. This is still a common disease.

Hepatitis

This is a virus that is most serious in very young dogs. It is spread by contact with an infected animal or its stool or urine. The virus affects the liver and kidneys and is characterized by high fever, depression and lack of appetite. Recovered animals may be afflicted with chronic illnesses.

Leptospirosis

This is a bacterial disease transmitted by contact with the urine of an infected dog, rat or other wildlife. It produces severe symptoms of fever, depression, jaundice and internal bleeding and was fatal before the vaccine was developed. Recovered dogs can be carriers, and the disease can be transmitted from dogs to humans.

Parvovirus

This was first noted in the late 1970s and is still a fatal disease. However, with proper vaccinations, early diagnosis and prompt treatment, it is a manageable disease. It attacks the bone marrow and intestinal tract. The symptoms include depression, loss of appetite, vomiting, diarrhea and collapse. Immediate medical attention is of the essence.

Bordetella attached to canine cilia. Otherwise known as kennel cough, this disease is highly contagious and should be vaccinated against routinely.

Rabies

This is shed in the saliva and is carried by raccoons, skunks, foxes, other dogs and cats. It attacks nerve tissue, resulting in paralysis and death. Rabies can be transmitted to people and is virtually always fatal. This disease is reappearing in the suburbs.

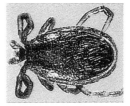

The deer tick is the most common carrier of Lyme disease. Photo courtesy of Virbac Laboratories, Inc., Fort Worth, Texas.

Bordetella (Kennel Cough)

The symptoms are coughing, sneezing, hacking and retching accompanied by nasal discharge usually lasting from a few days to several weeks. There are several disease-producing organisms responsible for this disease. The present vaccines are helpful but do not protect for all the strains. It usually is not life threatening but in some instances it can progress to a serious bronchopneumonia. The disease is highly contagious. The vaccination should be given routinely for dogs that come in contact with other dogs, such as through boarding, training class or visits to the groomer.

Coronavirus

This is usually self limiting and not life threatening. It was first noted in the late '70s about a year before parvovirus. The virus produces a yellow/brown stool and there may be depression, vomiting and diarrhea.

Lyme Disease

This was first diagnosed in the United States in 1976 in Lyme, CT in people who lived in close proximity to the deer tick. Symptoms may include acute lameness, fever, swelling of joints and loss of appetite. Your veterinarian can advise you if you live in an endemic area.

After your puppy has completed his puppy vaccinations, you will continue to booster the DHLPP once a year. It is customary to booster the rabies one year after the first vaccine and then, depending on where you live, it should be boostered every year or every three years. This depends on your local laws. The Lyme and corona vaccines are boostered annually and it is recommended that the bordetella be boostered every six to eight months.

Annual Visit

I would like to impress the importance of the annual check up, which would include the booster vaccinations, check for intestinal parasites and test for heartworm. Today in our very busy world it is rush, rush and see "how much you can get for how little." Unbelievably, some non-veterinary businesses have entered into the vaccination business. More harm than good can come to your dog through improper vaccinations, possibly from inferior vaccines and/or the wrong schedule. More than likely you truly care about your companion dog and over the years you have devoted much time and expense to his well being. Perhaps you are unaware that a vaccination is not just a vaccination. There is more involved. Please, please follow through with regular physical examinations. It is so important for your veterinarian to know your dog and this is especially true during middle age through the geriatric years. More than likely your older dog will require more than one physical a year. The annual physical is good preventive medicine. Through early diagnosis and subsequent treatment your dog can maintain a longer and better quality of life.

Intestinal Parasites

Hookworms

These are almost microscopic intestinal worms that can cause anemia and therefore serious problems, including death, in young puppies. Hookworms can be transmitted to humans through penetration of the skin. Puppies may be born with them.

Roundworms

These are spaghetti-like worms that can cause a potbellied appearance and dull coat along with more severe symptoms, such as vomiting, diarrhea and coughing. Puppies acquire these while in the mother's uterus and through lactation. Both hookworms and roundworms may be acquired through ingestion.

Whipworms

These have a three-month life cycle and are not acquired through the dam. They cause intermittent diarrhea usually with mucus. Whipworms are possibly the most difficult worm to eradicate. Their eggs are very resistant to most environmental factors and can last for years until the proper conditions enable them to mature. Whipworms are seldom seen in the stool.

Intestinal parasites are more prevalent in some areas than others. Climate, soil and contamination are big factors contributing to the incidence of intestinal parasites. Eggs are passed in the stool, lay on the ground and then become infective in a certain number of days. Each of the above worms has a different life cycle. Your best chance of becoming and remaining worm-free is to always pooper-scoop your yard. A fenced-in yard keeps stray dogs out, which is certainly helpful.

I would recommend having a fecal examination on your dog twice a year or more often if there is a problem. If your dog has a positive fecal sample, then he will be given the appropriate medication and you will be asked to bring back another stool sample in a certain period of time (depending on the type of worm) and then be rewormed.

Whipworms are hard to find unless one strains the feces, a job best left for a veterinarian.

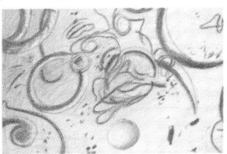

This process goes on until he has at least two negative samples. The different types of worms require different medications. You will be wasting your money and doing your dog an injustice by buying over-the-counter medication without first consulting your veterinarian.

OTHER INTERNAL PARASITES

Coccidiosis and Giardiasis

These protozoal infections usually affect puppies, especially in places where large numbers of puppies are brought together. Older dogs may harbor these infections but do not show signs unless they are stressed. Symptoms include diarrhea, weight loss and lack of appetite. These infections are not always apparent in the fecal examination.

Tapeworms

Seldom apparent on fecal floatation, they are diagnosed frequently as rice-like segments around the dog's anus and the base of the tail. Tapeworms are long, flat and ribbon like, sometimes several feet in length, and made up of many segments about five-eighths of an inch long. The two most common types of tapeworms found in the dog are:

(1) First the larval form of the flea tapeworm parasite must mature in an intermediate host, the flea, before it can become infective. Your dog acquires this by ingesting the flea through licking and chewing.

(2) Rabbits, rodents and certain large game animals serve as intermediate hosts for other species of tapeworms. If your dog should eat one of these infected hosts, then he can acquire tapeworms.

HEARTWORM DISEASE

This is a worm that resides in the heart and adjacent blood vessels of the lung that produces microfilaria, which circulate in the bloodstream. It is possible for a dog to be infected with any number of worms from one to a hundred that can be 6 to 14 inches long. It is a life-threatening disease, expensive to treat and easily prevented. Depending on where you live, your veterinarian may recommend a preventive year-round and either an annual or semiannual blood test. The most common preventive is given once a month.

EXTERNAL PARASITES

Fleas

These pests are not only the dog's worst enemy but also enemy to the owner's pocketbook. Preventing is less expensive than treating, but regardless I think we'd prefer to spend our money elsewhere. I would guess that the majority of our dogs are allergic to the bite of a flea, and in many cases it only takes one flea bite. The protein in the flea's saliva is the culprit. Allergic dogs have a reaction, which usually results in a "hot spot." More than likely such a reaction will involve a trip to the veterinarian for treatment. Yes, prevention is less expensive. Fortunately today there are several good products available.

If there is a flea infestation, no one product is going to correct the problem. Not only will the dog require treatment so will the environment. In general flea collars are not very effective although there is now available an "egg" collar that will kill the eggs on the dog. Dips are the most economical but they are messy. There are some effective shampoos and treatments available through pet shops and veterinarians. An oral tablet arrived on the American market in 1995 and was popular in Europe the previous year. It sterilizes the female flea but will not kill adult fleas. Therefore the tablet, which is given monthly, will decrease the flea population but is not a "cure-all." Those dogs that suffer from flea-bite allergy will still be subjected to the bite of the flea. Another popular parasiticide is permethrin, which is applied to the back of the dog in one or two places depending

Parasites like ticks can hide in grass, underbrush and low-lying trees. If you find any ticks on your Malamute, remove them promptly and carefully.

on the dog's weight. This product works as a repellent causing the flea to get "hot feet" and jump off. Do not confuse this product with some of the organophosphates that are also applied to the dog's back.

Some products are not usable on young puppies. Treating fleas should be done under your veterinarian's guidance. Frequently it is necessary to combine products and the layman does not have the knowledge regarding possible toxicities. It is hard to believe but there are a few dogs that do have a natural resistance to fleas. Nevertheless it would be wise to treat all pets at the same time. Don't forget your cats. Cats just love to prowl the neighborhood and consequently return with unwanted guests.

Adult fleas live on the dog but their eggs drop off the dog into the environment. There they go through four larval stages before reaching adulthood, and thereby are able to jump back on the poor unsuspecting dog. The cycle resumes and takes between 21 to 28 days under ideal conditions. There are environmental products available that will kill both the adult fleas and the larvae.

Ticks

Ticks carry Rocky Mountain Spotted Fever, Lyme disease and can cause tick paralysis. They should be removed with tweezers, trying to pull out the head. The jaws carry disease. There is a tick preventive collar that does an excellent job. The ticks automatically back out on those dogs wearing collars.

Sarcoptic Mange

This is a mite that is difficult to find on skin scrapings. The pinnal reflex is a good indicator of this disease. Rub the ends of the pinna (ear) together and the dog will start scratching with

Be sure to check your Malamute's coat thoroughly after he has been outdoors for fleas, ticks or any other foreign matter such as burrs or thorns.

his foot. Sarcoptes are highly contagious to other dogs and to humans although they do not live long on humans. They cause intense itching.

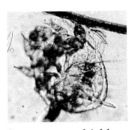

Demodectic Mange

This is a mite that is passed from the dam to her puppies. It affects youngsters age three to ten months. Diagnosis is confirmed by skin scraping. Small areas of alopecia around the eyes, lips and/or forelegs become visible. There is little itching unless there is a secondary bacterial infection. Some breeds are afflicted more than others.

Sarcoptes are highly contagious to other dogs and to humans, although they do not live long on humans, but are itchy.

Cheyletiella

This causes intense itching and is diagnosed by skin scraping. It lives in the outer layers of the skin of dogs, cats, rabbits and humans. Yellow-gray scales may be found on the back and the rump, top of the head and the nose.

To Breed or Not To Breed

More than likely your breeder has requested that you have your puppy neutered or spayed. Your breeder's request is based on what is healthiest for your dog and what is most beneficial for your breed. Experienced and conscientious breeders devote many years into developing a bloodline. In order to do this, he makes every effort to plan each breeding in regard to conformation, temperament and health. This type of breeder does his best to perform the necessary testing (i.e., OFA, CERF, testing for inherited blood disorders, thyroid, etc.). Testing is expensive and sometimes very disheartening when a favorite dog doesn't pass his health tests. The health history pertains not only to the breeding stock but to the immediate ancestors. Reputable breeders do not want their offspring to be bred indiscriminately. Therefore you may be asked to neuter or spay your puppy. Of course there is always the exception, and your breeder may agree to let you breed your dog under his direct supervision. This is an important concept. More and more effort is being made to breed healthier dogs.

Spay/Neuter

There are numerous benefits of performing this surgery at six months of age. Unspayed females are subject to mammary and ovarian cancer. In order to prevent mammary cancer she must be spayed prior to her first heat cycle. Later in life, an unspayed female may develop a pyometra (an infected uterus), which is definitely life threatening.

Spaying is performed under a general anesthetic and is easy on the young dog. As you might expect it is a little harder on the older dog, but that is no reason to deny her the surgery. The surgery removes the ovaries and uterus. It is important to remove all the ovarian tissue. If some is left behind, she could remain attractive to males. In order to view the ovaries, a reasonably long incision is necessary. An ovariohysterectomy is considered major surgery.

Neutering the male at a young age will inhibit some characteristic male behavior that owners frown upon. I have found my boys will not hike their legs and mark territory if they are neutered at six months of age. Also neutering at a young age has hormonal benefits, lessening the chance of hormonal aggressiveness.

Surgery involves removing the testicles but leaving the scrotum. If there should be a retained testicle, then he definitely needs to be neutered before the age of two or three years. Retained testicles can develop into cancer. Unneutered males are at risk for testicular cancer, perineal fistulas, perianal tumors and fistulas and prostatic disease.

Intact males and females are prone to housebreaking accidents. Females urinate frequently before, during and after heat cycles, and males tend to mark territory if there is a female in heat. Males may show the same behavior if there is a visiting dog or guests.

Surgery involves a sterile operating procedure equivalent to human surgery. The incision site is shaved, surgically scrubbed and draped. The veterinarian

Breeding should only be done by someone who is conscientious, knowledgeable and willing to take responsibility for the dogs and new puppies involved.

Spaying/neutering is often the best option for your Malamute pet. It will minimize the risk of certain diseases of the reproductive system and prevent unwanted litters.

wears a sterile surgical gown, cap, mask and gloves. Anesthesia should be monitored by a registered technician. It is customary for the veterinarian to recommend a pre-anesthetic blood screening, looking for metabolic problems and a ECG rhythm strip to check for normal heart function. Today anesthetics are equal to human anesthetics, which enables your dog to walk out of the clinic the same day as surgery.

Some folks worry about their dog gaining weight after being neutered or spayed. This is usually not the case. It is true that some dogs may be less active so they could develop a problem, but my own dogs are just as active as they were before surgery. I have a hard time keeping weight on them. However, if your dog should begin to gain, then you need to decrease his food and see to it that he gets a little more exercise.

MEDICAL PROBLEMS

Anal Sacs

These are small sacs on either side of the rectum that can

cause the dog discomfort when they are full. They should empty when the dog has a bowel movement. Symptoms of inflammation or impaction are excessive licking under the tail and/or a bloody or sticky discharge from the anal area. Breeders like myself recommend emptying the sacs on a regular schedule when bathing the dog. Many veterinarians prefer this isn't done unless there are symptoms. You can express the sacs by squeezing the two sacs (at the five and seven o'clock positions) in and up toward the anus. Take precautions not to get in the way of the foul-smelling fluid that is expressed. Some dogs object to this procedure so it would be wise to have someone hold the head. Scooting is caused by anal-sac irritation and not worms.

This young Alaskan Malamute pup has a lot of potential! Proper health care right from the start will ensure that he is able to lead a full and active life.

Colitis

The stool may be frank blood or blood tinged and is the result of inflammation of the colon. Colitis, sometimes intermittent, can be the result of stress, undiagnosed whipworms, or perhaps idiopathic (no explainable reason). I have had several dogs prone to this disorder. They felt fine and were willing to eat but would have intermittent bloody stools. If this in an ongoing problem, you should probably feed a diet higher in fiber. Seek professional help if your dog feels poorly and/or the condition persists.

Conjunctivitis

Many breeds are prone to this problem. The conjunctiva is the pink tissue that lines the inner surface of the eyeball except the clear, transparent cornea. Irritating substances such as bacteria, foreign matter or chemicals can cause it to become reddened and swollen. It is important to keep any hair trimmed from around the eyes. Long hair stays damp and aggravates the problem. Keep the eyes cleaned with warm water and wipe away any matter that has accumulated in the corner of the eyes. If the condition persists, you should see your veterinarian. This problem goes hand in hand with keratoconjunctivitis sicca.

DENTAL CARE for Your Dog's Life

S o you've got a new puppy! You also have a new set of puppy teeth in your household. Anyone who has ever raised a puppy is abundantly aware of these new teeth. Your puppy will chew anything it can reach, chase your shoelaces, and play "tear the rag" with any piece of clothing it can find. When puppies are newly born, they have no teeth. At about four weeks of age, puppies of most breeds begin to develop their deciduous or baby teeth. They

Make sure your Malamute has a safe Nylabone® to play with to satisfy his chewing needs. Adults enjoy Nylabones® as much as developing puppies.

begin eating semi-solid food, fighting and biting with their litter mates, and learning discipline from their mother. As their new teeth come in, they inflict more pain on their mother's breasts, so her feeding

Your Alaskan Malamute will be happier and his teeth and gums healthier if you give him a Souper-sized POPpup™ to chew on. Every POPpup™ is 100% edible and enhanced with dog-friendly ingredients like liver, cheese, spinach, chicken, carrots or potatoes.

sessions become less frequent and shorter. By six or eight weeks, the mother will start growling to warn her pups when they are fighting too roughly or hurting her as they nurse too much with their new teeth.

Puppies need to chew. It is a necessary part of their physical and mental development. They develop muscles and necessary life skills as they drag objects around, fight over possession, and vocalize alerts and warnings. Puppies chew on things to explore their world. They are using their sense of taste to determine what is food and what is not. How else can they tell an electrical cord from a lizard? At about four months of age, most puppies begin shedding their baby teeth. Often these teeth need some help to come out and make way for the permanent teeth. The incisors (front teeth) will be replaced first. Then, the adult canine or fang teeth erupt. When the baby tooth is not shed before the permanent tooth comes in, veterinarians call it a retained deciduous tooth. This condition will often cause gum infections by trapping hair and debris between the permanent tooth and the retained baby tooth. Nylafloss® is an excellent device for puppies to use. They can toss it, drag it, and chew on the many surfaces it presents. The baby teeth can catch in

the nylon material, aiding in their removal. Puppies that have adequate chew toys will have less destructive behavior, develop more physically, and have less chance of retained deciduous teeth.

During the first year, your dog should be seen by your veterinarian at regular intervals. Your veterinarian will let you know when to bring in your puppy for vaccinations and parasite examinations. At each visit, your veterinarian should inspect the lips, teeth, and mouth as part of a complete physical examination. You should take some part in the maintenance of your dog's oral health. You should examine your dog's mouth weekly throughout his first year to make sure there are no sores, foreign objects, tooth problems, etc. If your dog drools excessively, shakes its head, or has bad breath, consult your veterinarian. By the time your dog is six months old, the permanent teeth are all in and plaque can start to accumulate on the tooth surfaces. This is when your dog needs to develop good dental-care habits to prevent calculus build-up on its teeth. Brushing is best. That is a fact that cannot be denied. However, some dogs do not like their teeth brushed regularly, or you may not be able to accomplish the task. In that case, you should consider a product that will help prevent plaque and calculus build-up.

The Plaque Attackers® and Galileo Bone® are other excellent choices for the first three years of a dog's life. Their shapes make them interesting for the dog. As the dog chews on them, the solid polyurethane massages the gums which improves the blood

As a pet owner, it is essential to keep your dog's teeth clean by removing surface tartar and plaque. 2-Brush® by Nylabone® is made with two toothbrushes to clean both sides of your Malamute's teeth at the same time. Each brush contains a reservoir designed to apply the toothpaste, which is specially formulated for dogs, directly into the toothbrush.

Give your Alaskan Malamute good dental care throughout his life and he will always be able to flash a healthy smile!

circulation to the periodontal tissues. Projections on the chew devices increase the surface and are in contact with the tooth for more efficient cleaning. The unique shape and consistency prevent your dog from exerting excessive force on his own teeth or from breaking off pieces of the bone. If your dog is an aggressive chewer or weighs more than 55 pounds (25 kg), you should consider giving him a Nylabone®, the most durable chew product on the market.

The Gumabones ®, made by the Nylabone Company, are constructed of strong polyurethane, which is softer than nylon. Less powerful chewers prefer the Gumabones® to the Nylabones®. A super option for your dog is the Hercules Bone®, a uniquely shaped bone named after the great Olympian for its exception strength. Like all Nylabone products, they are specially scented to make them attractive to your dog. Ask your veterinarian about these bones and he will validate the good doctor's prescription: Nylabones® not only give your dog a good chewing workout but also help to save your dog's teeth (and even his life, as it protects him from possible fatal periodontal diseases).

By the time dogs are four years old, 75% of them have periodontal disease. It is the most common infection in dogs. Yearly examinations by your veterinarian are essential to maintaining your dog's good

Let your Alaskan Malamute do his part in keeping his teeth clean by allowing him to chew on a Carrot Bone™ by Nylabone®. It is a healthy chew containing no plastic or artificial ingredients.

Roar-Hide® by Nylabone® is the safe alternative to traditional rawhide. It is melted and molded so it will not break up into harmful pieces and it is 86.2% protein.

health. If your veterinarian detects periodontal disease, he or she may recommend a prophylactic cleaning. To do a thorough cleaning, it will be necessary to put your dog under anesthesia. With modern gas anesthetics and monitoring equipment, the procedure is pretty safe. Your veterinarian will scale the teeth with an ultrasound scaler or hand instrument. This removes the calculus from the teeth. If there are calculus deposits below the gum line, the veterinarian will plane the roots to make them smooth. After all of the calculus has been removed, the teeth are polished with pumice in a polishing cup. If any medical or surgical treatment is needed, it is done at this time. The final step would be fluoride treatment and your follow-up treatment at home. If the periodontal disease is advanced, the veterinarian may prescribe a medicated mouth rinse or antibiotics for use at home. Make sure your dog has safe, clean and attractive chew toys and treats. Chooz® treats are another way of using a consumable treat to help keep your dog's teeth clean.

Rawhide is the most popular of all materials for a dog to chew. This has never been good news to dog owners, because rawhide is inherently very dangerous for dogs. Thousands of dogs have died from rawhide, having swallowed the hide after it has become soft and mushy, only to cause stomach and intestinal blockage. A new rawhide product on the market has finally solved the problem of rawhide: molded Roar-Hide® from Nylabone. These are composed of processed, cut up, and melted American rawhide injected into your dog's favorite shape: a dog bone. These dog-safe devices smell and taste like rawhide but don't break up. The ridges on the bones help to fight tartar build-up on the teeth and they last ten times longer than the usual rawhide chews.

Give your Malamute a Plaque Attacker™ by Nylabone®. The raised tips are specifically designed to combat plaque and tartar build-up.

As your dog ages, professional examination and cleaning should become more frequent. The mouth should be inspected at least once a year. Your veterinarian may recommend visits every six months. In the geriatric patient, organs such as the heart, liver, and kidneys do not function as well as when they were young. Your veterinarian will probably want to test these organs' functions prior to using general anesthesia for dental cleaning. If your dog is a good chewer and you work closely with your veterinarian, your dog can keep all of its teeth all of its life. However, as your dog ages, his sense of smell, sight, and taste will diminish. He may not have the desire to chase, trap or chew his toys. He will also not have the energy to chew for long periods, as arthritis and periodontal disease make chewing painful. This will leave you with more responsibility for keeping his teeth clean and healthy. The dog that would not let you brush his teeth at one year of age, may let you brush his teeth now that he is ten years old.

If you train your dog with good chewing habits as a puppy, he will have healthier teeth throughout his life.

Make sure your Alaskan Malamute puppy has safe toys to chew on. Cotton tug toys may rot or break into pieces that can be swallowed.

IDENTIFICATION and Finding the Lost Dog

by Judy Iby

There are several ways of identifying your dog. The old standby is a collar with dog license, rabies, and ID tags. Unfortunately collars have a way of being separated from the dog and tags fall off. I am not suggesting you shouldn't use a collar and tags. If they stay intact and on the dog, they are the quickest way of identification.

For several years owners have been tattooing their dogs. Some tattoos use a number with a registry. Here lies the problem because there are several registries to check. If you wish to tattoo, use your social security number.

"Denali" is ready to go! This enthusiastic girl has an obedience title, is a conformation champion and is a top weight pulling competitor, having pulled just under 2500 pounds.

The humane shelters have the means to trace it. It is usually done on the inside of the rear thigh. The area is first shaved and numbed. There is no pain, although a few dogs do not like the buzzing sound. Occasionally tattooing is not legible and needs to be redone.

The newest method of identification is microchipping. The microchip is a computer chip that is no larger than a grain of rice. The veterinarian implants it by injection between the shoulder blades. The dog feels no discomfort. If your dog is lost and picked up by the humane society, they can trace you

by scanning the microchip, which has its own code. Microchip scanners are friendly to other brands of microchips and their

To keep your Alaskan Malamute from wandering, your yard should be securely fenced.

registries. The microchip comes with a dog tag saying the dog is microchipped. It is the safest way of identifying your dog.

FINDING THE LOST DOG

I am sure you will agree with me that there would be little worse than losing your dog. Responsible pet owners rarely lose their dogs. They do not let their dogs run free because they don't want harm to come to them. Not only that but in most, if not all, states there is a leash law.

Below is a list that hopefully will be of help to you if you need it. Remember don't give up, keep looking. Your dog is worth your efforts.

1. Contact your neighbors and put flyers with a photo on it in their mailboxes. Information you should include would be the dog's name, breed, sex, color, age, source of identification, when your dog was last seen and where, and your name and phone numbers. It may be helpful to say the dog needs medical care. Offer a *reward*.
2. Check all local shelters daily. It is also possible for your dog to be picked up away from home and end up in an out-of-the-way shelter. Check these too. Go in person. It is not good enough to call. Most shelters are limited on the time they can hold dogs then they are put up for adoption or euthanized. There is the possibility that your dog will not make it to the shelter for several days. Your dog could have been wandering or someone may have tried to keep him.
3. Notify all local veterinarians. Call and send flyers.
4. Call your breeder. Frequently breeders are contacted when one of their breed is found.
5. Contact the rescue group for your breed.
6. Contact local schools—children may have seen your dog.
7. Post flyers at the schools, groceries, gas stations, convenience stores, veterinary clinics, groomers and any other place that will allow them.
8. Advertise in the newspaper.
9. Advertise on the radio.

SUGGESTED READING

PS-737
This Is The Alaskan Malamute
Joan McDonald Brearly
415 pages.

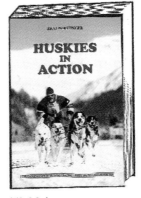

TS-234
Huskies in Action
Rico Pfirststinger
140 pages, over 120 full color photos.

TS-257
Choosing A Dog For Life
Andrew DePrisco
384 pages,over 800 full color photos.

TS-258
Training Your Dog For Sports and Other Activities
Charlotte Schwartz
160 pages, over 200 full color photos.

INDEX

Adolescence, 53
Aggression, 123
Agility, 107
Alaska, 11, 15
Alaska Geographic Quarterly, 14
Alaskan Malamute Club of America, 14, 55
Alaskan Malamute Club, 14
Alaskan Malamute Protection League, 54, 55
American Kennel Club, 14, 91, 109
Anal sacs, 146
Bannister, Henry, M., 14
Barking, 126
Bering Strait, 11
Bering, Vitus, 12
Biting, 128
Body language, 119
Bordetella, 137
Busch, Robert H., 6
Bustad Buddies Program, 88
Bustad, Leo Dr., 88
Canadian Kennel Club, 91
Canine Eye Registration Foundation (CERF), 138
Canine Good Citizen Test, 103
Cataracts, 38
Chewing, 148
Cheyletiella, 143
Chinook Kennels, 15
Chondrodysplasia, 38
Coccidiosis, 139
Colitis, 146
Collars, 156
Come, 79
Conformation, 94
Conjunctivitis, 146
Coronavirus, 137
Crates, 74, 75
−training, 74
Demodectic mange, 143
Diet sheet, 49
Digging, 129

Distemper, 134, 135
Dog food, 58
Dogs of Great Britain, America and Other Countries, The, 12
Down, 82, 93
Dwarfism, 38
Exercise, 68
Fear, 122
Fleas, 140
Food, 56, 57
−puppy, 56
−diet sheet, 49
Giardiasis, 139
Grooming, 66
Guiffre, Martha, 15
Health guarantee, 50
Health record, 47
Heartworm disease, 140
Heel, 84, 93
Hepatitis, 134
Hip dysplasia, 38
Hookworms, 138
Housebreaking, 74
Identification papers, 47
Immunizations, 39, 134
−puppy, 39
Jumping up, 127
Junior Showmanship, 102
Kendrick, William, 15
Kennel Club, The, 91, 98
Kennel cough, 137
Klondike Gold Rush, 14
Leash training, 77, 78
Leptospirosis, 134
Lyme disease, 137
Mahlemut Indians, 11, 12
Mange, 142
−cheyletiella, 143
−demodectic, 143
−sarcoptic, 142
Microchipping, 156
Natural History of Dogs, The, 6
Neutering, 144
Nutrition, 56
Obedience, 104
Obedience matches, 105
Orthopedic Foundation for Animals (OFA), 143

Parainfluenza, 134
Parvovirus, 134
Pedigree, 48
People-Pet Partnership, 88
Performance tests, 108
Periodontal disease, 152
Pet Awareness Week, 112
Pullman Memorial Hospital, 88
Puppy, 16
−coat, 18, 62
−diet, 56
−selection, 16
−socialization, 18, 19
Puppy kindergarten, 92
Rabies, 137
Rawhide, 153
Recall, 94
Registration certificate, 48
Roundworms, 138
Sarcoptic mange, 142
Seeley, Eva, 15
Shallbetter, Allen and Sandy, 88
Sit, 80, 92
Skijorring, 88
Sledding, 88
Socialization, 50, 70, 116
−puppy, 18, 19
Spaying, 144
Stay, 80
Stonehenge, 12
Supplementation, 60
Tapeworms, 140
Tattooing, 156
Temperament, 50
Ticks, 142
Tracking, 106
Training, 76
−classes, 87
−crate, 74
−obedience, 104
Vaccinations, 135
Veterinarian, 131
−annual visit, 139
−check up, 130
−physical exam, 131
von Kotzebue, Otto, 12
Whipworms, 138